# Trout Dreams

A GALLERY OF FLY-FISHING PROFILES

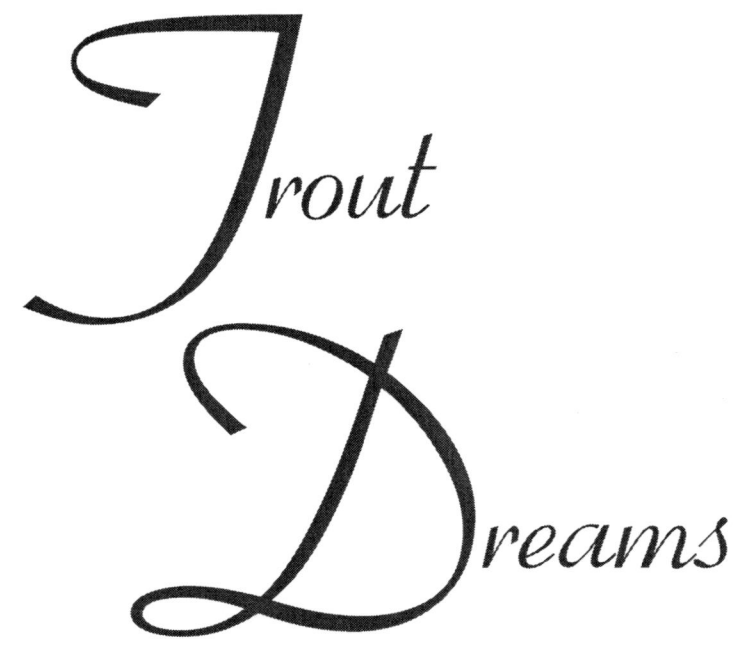

# Trout Dreams

~ J. I. MERRITT ~

# THE DERRYDALE PRESS

## LANHAM AND NEW YORK

## THE DERRYDALE PRESS

Published in the United States of America by
The Derrydale Press
4720 Boston Way, Lanham, Maryland 20706

Distributed by NATIONAL BOOK NETWORK, INC.

Photograph for chapter 1 courtesy of Barry Staver; photographs for chapters 2, 3, 4, 5, 6, 9, and 10 courtesy of Jim Merritt; photograph for chapter 7 courtesy of Al Troth; photograph for chapter 8 courtesy of Ed Black; photograph for chapter 11 courtesy of Jim Watt and Kelly Watt; photograph for chapter 12 courtesy of Debie Waterman; photograph for chapter 13 courtesy of Bill Smith; photograph for chapter 14 courtesy of Joel Snyder.

British Library Cataloguing in Publication Information Available

**Library of Congress Cataloging-in-Publication Data**

Merritt, J. I.
    Trout dreams : a gallery of fly-fishing profiles / by J. I. Merritt.
      p. cm.
    Includes bibliographical references.
    ISBN 1-58667-011-5 (cloth : alk. paper)
    1. Fishers—United States—Biography. 2. Trout fishing—United States—Anecdotes. I. Title.

SH20.A1 M47   2000
799.1'092'273—dc21
[B]                                     00-035843

♾™ The paper used in this publication meets the minimum requirements of American National Standard for Information Sciences—Permanence of Paper for Printed Library Materials, ANSI/NISO Z39.48-1992.
Manufactured in the United States of America.

*To Peter Longstreth,*
*the better nympher*

# Contents

# Introduction

*The Trout is a fish highly valued . . . a generous*
*fish . . . a fish that feeds clean and purely, in*
*the swiftest streams, and on the hardest gravel.*
—Izaak Walton

I don't remember my first trout, although I do know that it was a cutthroat and that I caught it in the summer of 1970 on Sunlight Creek, in the Absaroka Mountains east of Yellowstone National Park. I might have been—OK, I almost certainly was—fishing with a worm, and I am fairly certain that my tackle was a spinning outfit borrowed from my father-in-law, Ned Russell of St. Louis. Ned had brought his entire family to the 7D Ranch near Cody, Wyoming, and our two weeks there were my introduction to trout fishing and the Rocky Mountain West. At some point during our stay Ned also let me borrow his fly rod, and despite my ungainly casting I was able to catch a few more cutts—on worms and grasshoppers but also on a Muddler Minnow. Not one of these sleek little torpedoes, with green spotted backs and a slash of orange under their jaws, was bigger than ten or twelve inches. Their wild beauty left a deep impression.

Raised in the suburbs of New York City, I had no fishing experience to speak of before that summer. I had always associated fish with lakes, and it took me a while to adjust to the realization that they could live in swift mountain streams. An even stranger notion was that insects—mayflies, caddis flies, and stone flies—lived in the same streams and that trout fed on them.

My literal immersion in this mysterious world was the start of a lifetime's preoccupation. My chosen career of journalism soon added a dimension to my fly-fishing, and as an occasional outdoor writer I have been able to profile some of the sport's more influential or engaging characters. *Trout Dreams* is a baker's dozen of such portraits, adapted from articles published between 1981 and 1997. Since the pieces on them appeared, a couple of my subjects (Dan Bailey and Chuck Fothergill) have passed beyond the bar. Although their backgrounds vary, the anglers chronicled here are united by the same compulsion to make their fly-fishing something more than an avocation. Most channeled their passion for salmonids into a living—as shop owners (Bailey, Fran Betters), flytiers or guides (Fothergill, Al Troth), entrepreneurs (Dennis Black), filmmakers (Jim and Kelly Watt), or teachers (Joe Humphreys). Some, like Al Caucci (an author, entomologist, fly-tying innovator, and camp owner), Bill Yellowtail (a rancher, politician, and guide), and "Colonial Angler" Ken Reinard can't be so neatly pigeonholed.

Most of my subjects have affected fly-fishing in one way or another, a few of them significantly. Dan Bailey pioneered the fly-fishing mail-order catalog business and, through his friendship with writers such as Joe Brooks and Charley Waterman, he did much to popularize western fishing. As a Montana state senator, Bill Yellowtail spearheaded legislation that assured anglers of continued access to his state's blue-ribbon trout fisheries. Dennis Black, the founder of Umpqua Feather Merchants, helped fuel fly-fishing's booming popularity in the 1980s by meeting the demand for high-quality flies at reasonable prices, while his strategy of setting up fly factories overseas brought fly-fishing into the global economy. That same economy has benefited from Jim and Kelly Watts's promotion of destination angling through their *Fly-fishing Video Magazine,* whose overall quality set a standard for a genre that for a time seemed terminally afflicted with amateuritis.

At the other end of the spectrum from Dennis Black is Al Troth, a traditional, cottage-industry flytier whose principal creation, the Elk-Hair Caddis, is a staple of most anglers' fly boxes. Two of my other subjects, Al Caucci and Fran Betters, are the father and godfather, respectively, of the popular Comparadun series of dry flies. Along with his partner Bob Nastasi, Caucci has also created enduring, user-friendly systems for tying flies and identifying trout stream insects.

Less tangible but no less real is the contribution that Norman Maclean made through his great novella, *A River Runs through It*—a story of love, loss, and redemption built around his family's relationship with the Blackfoot River. Maclean's tale teaches us about the connectedness of fly-fishing with the rest of life. It is a book that at some deep level has redefined the collective consciousness of our "sport," indeed, that makes the very term seem trivial.

I've learned something from all my subjects. Occasionally the lessons were technical (as in Chuck Fothergill's "outrigger" nymphing), but more often they were philosophical. I think particularly of Dan Bailey and Charley Waterman, two of the least affected people I've ever met. Their low-key approach to angling suggests that fishing "success" bears little relation to the number and size of fish caught but has everything to do with attitude.

One criterion for inclusion in *Trout Dreams* was that I actually fished with my subjects or at least observed them fishing—a rule I stretched in the case of Maclean and Waterman and also, of course, Silas Goodrich, the ace angler on the Lewis and Clark expedition.

For their encouragement and guidance, my thanks to editors Silvio Calabi, John Merwin, and Jim Butler at *Fly Rod & Reel* and to Duncan Barnes, Maggie Nichols, Dave Petzal, and Slaton White at *Field & Stream*.

## ONE

## A Fish for Dan Bailey

Dan Bailey's fly shop in Livingston, Montana, didn't look like a leading American corporation, and its laid-back proprietor scarcely fit the image of an industrial tycoon.

As it did when I first visited Bailey's in 1981, and as it does today, the shop sits across the railroad tracks between Gil's Got It (a gift store) and the local Chevrolet dealership. Its green stucco exterior was as unassuming as I found Bailey himself, a former physicist. Forty-five years earlier he had quit a teaching job in Brooklyn, New York, to move to Montana and devote his life to trout fishing on the Yellowstone River. In time, the tackle business that he started in order to support himself and his family between fishing trips grew into the largest manufacturer of flies in the United States. In the small but select world of fly-fishing, both the shop and its founder were institutions.

It was August—prime season on the Yellowstone, which often remains high with runoff through mid-July—and I found it buzzing with fishermen amid racks of rods, boots, hats, and other angling paraphernalia, including examples of some five hundred fly patterns arrayed in compartments along a room-length counter. I spotted the seventy-seven-year-old Bailey—a small, wiry man in a checked shirt—at his cluttered desk behind the counter, answering the constantly ringing phone with a laconic "Dan here," or pecking away at a venerable typewriter as he turned out an inimitably folksy letter to one of his 50,000 mail-order customers. The recipients often framed them.

The heart of the business, the fly-tying operation, was in an adjoining room, where rows of women tiers spun fur and feathers into popular Bailey patterns such as the Royal Wulff, Muddler Minnow, and Goofus Bug. The shop's thirty tiers, I learned, turned out some 750,000 flies a year for customers in all fifty states and thirty-six foreign countries. He traditionally employed women tiers, and the walls of the tying room were decorated with posters of Elvis, Burt Reynolds, and other male heartthrobs. Bailey's "girls," almost none of whom had ever fished, learned tying in two to six months under the watchful eye of master tier Louise Monical. Some of them had worked there for decades, tying a single pattern for years at a time. They were paid by the piece, and an experienced tier could produce up to fourteen dozen flies a day.

A testimonial to the effectiveness of Bailey flies is the Wall of Fame, which then as now dominates the main part of the shop. For a few of the thousands of angling pilgrims who wend their way each year to Bailey's and the brawling Yellowstone beyond its doors, beatitude is having one of their fish enshrined amid the panorama of more than three hundred wooden plaques lining the shop walls, each sporting the outline of a trout four pounds or over taken from the waters around Livingston.

My entree to Bailey came through assignments from *Rod & Reel* and *People* magazines. (I had persuaded the editors at *People* that Bailey was worthy of a story by pointing out that a scene from the cult film classic *Rancho Deluxe,* based on a screenplay by Tom McGuane, had been shot in the fly shop.) Bailey had recently been the subject of a profile in *Quest* magazine, and in another month, I learned, he would be answering questions for the cameras of ABC-TV's *Good Morning America.* After more than four decades in the business, Dan Bailey had suddenly found himself a walking media event, and he could only scratch his bald pate and grin in amazement. Why all the fuss over an ex-Kentucky farm boy who liked to do some fishing?

Bailey's Huck Finn origins belied a keen intelligence and a business shrewdness unsurpassed among major tackle dealers of his day. He grew up on a farm near Russellville, in southwestern Kentucky. By age seven he was catching farm-pond

crappies on worms dangled from a cane pole. Under the guidance of an angling uncle ("my father always worked too hard
to have time to fish," he told me) he soon owned a fly rod and
was taking smallmouth on flies he had tied himself.

Dan showed an aptitude for science and, after graduating
in 1926 from The Citadel (this most unmilitary of men),
earned a master's degree in physics at the University of Kentucky. It was during a year's teaching stint at Jefferson City Junior College, Missouri, that he first fished for trout, at Bennett
Springs in the Ozarks. A second teaching job, this one at
Lehigh University, put him close to some of the best trout
country in the East. In 1930 he moved to New York City to
teach at Brooklyn Polytechnic Institute and pursue a Ph.D. in
physics at New York University.

Bailey spent six years in the urban canyons of New York.
He made friends with *Fortune* writer John McDonald and a
commercial artist named Lee Wulff, and on weekends the three
of them explored the Beaverkill, the Ausable, and other famous
streams of the Catskills and Adirondacks. Dan's acquaintances
included Catskill flytiers Harry Darbee, Walt Dette, and Reuben
Cross, and it was not too long before he began tying his own
flies commercially. Eventually he and Wulff opened a fly tying
school in a room behind Lee Chumley's Restaurant in Greenwich Village. Their one student was a corporate lawyer named
John J. McCloy, who would later become U.S. High Commis-
sioner in postwar Germany and an adviser to eight American

presidents from Roosevelt to Carter. He remained a Bailey customer for fifty years.

The origin of the Wall of Fame goes back to Bailey's New York years, when he shared a fishing cabin on a tributary to Roundout Creek in the Catskills with Ivan Bloch, another city friend and the son of composer Ernest Bloch. "Whenever one of us caught a big trout we'd trace its outline right on the wall," he recalled. "Later on, after I came out here, I had the notion it would be an attractive idea for the shop. At first we drew them on the wallpaper, then we got a little fancier and put them on boards." Each silhouette on the Wall of Fame is spotted with the symbolic colors of a brown, rainbow, or cutthroat trout; lettering below the silhouette indicates the place and date where the trout was caught, the fly used, and the angler's name. One of the larger fish represented is a six-pound brown taken from the Yellowstone on August 26, 1965, on a Mizoolian Spook. The angler: Dan Bailey.

It was through Ivan Bloch that Dan met the woman who would become his wife. Helen Bailey, a born-and-bred Manhattanite, was living in Greenwich Village at the time and working for the city as a public health nurse. Dan introduced Helen to fly-fishing, and her adeptness with a dry fly soon became the talk of their Catskill angling circle. They married in 1936.

Looking for ways to supplement their modest income, Helen convinced Dan to tie huge decorative flies of gaudy feathers and tinsel for ladies' hats at Bergdorf Goodman, a tony Manhattan department store. (Bailey received ten cents apiece for his real flies and a dollar each for the outsized variety.) Their friend John McDonald, who would become a preeminent angling scholar with books on Dame Juliana Berners's *A Treatise of Fishing with an Angle* and Theodore Gordon (the tubercular, reclusive father of dry-fly-fishing in America), wrote a memorable account of Bailey's venture into the millinery trade, in which McDonald reported casting one of the Bergdorf creations on a Catskill pool and watching the water explode with the biggest brown trout he'd ever seen.

For their honeymoon the Baileys went west to Montana, where Dan was eager to try the fishing. He liked it so much that they came out again the next year, with Dan staying behind to scout out more streams while Helen returned to her nursing job in New York. Although close to obtaining his doctorate, Dan by now had decided to abandon plans for an academic career. His field had been atomic physics. "I got out just before it started to get popular," he said, with no trace of regret. "The job prospects were pretty much limited to teaching at the time, and I saw that I wasn't going to be an Einstein."

Instead, he had unilaterally determined to settle in the West and make a living of sorts tying flies. "There was no use resisting," Helen said. "When we said good-bye to our friends in New York, people looked at us as if we were crazy. We had no money, and of course, who'd ever heard of Montana?" Having narrowed their choice of where to live between Bozeman and Livingston, Dan settled on the latter literally by accident. Driving over Bozeman Pass one day, Helen went off the road and damaged the car's axle. The Baileys limped into Livingston, and while waiting for repairs Dan decided he'd found his nirvana.

"I wanted to be in the best place for fishing in the United States," he recalled. "I'd already worked up a little mail-order business with flies and figured I could set up a shop and make a living. We rented rooms in the old Albemarle Hotel. I started tying flies, persuaded a few companies to give me credit on equipment, and started in the tackle business."

Although Helen found work as a school nurse, cash flow remained a problem. To help pay the bills Dan resorted to various gambits: for a time the fly shop doubled as a shooting gallery, and he also wholesaled whitefish until one Christmas vacation, when the man left in charge of the business was jailed for nonsupport and hundreds of pounds of fish flesh rotted in the shop.

When I met the Baileys they had been in Livingston, a railroad town of 7,500 with more bars than churches, since 1938. For the last fourteen years, home had been a contemporary house on Loch Levin Drive (named, appropriately, for one of the two strains of brown trout, a European species, introduced into the United States in the 1880s). They shared the house with a pair of black labs named Peter and Mittie, and from the living room they looked through sliding glass doors to soaring cottonwoods and Livingston Peak in the distance. The Yellowstone River ran only a stone's throw from the house, and the Bailey patio fronted on a spring-fed lagoon holding brown, brook, rainbow, and cutthroat trout. Dan kept a fly rod rigged for any guest who might want to have a go at the spooky two-plus pounders cruising in plain view from the patio. Although seldom fishing for these monsters himself, on our visit to the Bailey home he was asked by the *People* photographer to make a few casts. Dan demurred at first—he didn't want anyone thinking this was how he usually fished—but was persuaded to give it a try. To his genuine chagrin, on the third cast he hooked, then played and released, a nineteen-inch rainbow. An hour later, again at the photographer's request, he repeated the performance with an eighteen-inch brook trout fooled on the first cast. I could only conclude that Dan Bailey could not help catching fish, even when he would rather not.

In the living room, we sipped bourbon while the Baileys reminisced some about the early days with the shop. "The Depression was an easier time to start a business like this than would be the case today," Dan said. "Nobody had any money, so there was never much business, but interest rates were low, credit was easy, and you could start with a bare minimum."

Helen recalled, however, that Dan never let business interfere with what really mattered. "Sometimes," she said, "Dan would put a sign on the door—gone fishing—when he still had orders to fill. I'd be furious. I tried helping in the shop for a while, but it didn't work out. That's when I decided that he'd go his way and I'd go mine, and we'd be very happy."

Bailey's became an established tackle operation after World War II, its success spurred by endorsements from national fishing writers like Ray Bergman and Joe Brooks. "Dan was an especially soft sell—everybody liked him—and he became accepted as an angling authority," fishing writer and Livingston resident Charley Waterman, a longtime Bailey friend, told me later. "Most editors twenty or thirty years ago wouldn't let you mention a fly shop in an article, but they'd let you write about Bailey's." His customer relations were special too, Waterman added. "If you wrote Dan Bailey a letter asking about some item of tackle or conditions on the Yellowstone, you'd get a personally typed letter back from Bailey—and no one else was doing anything like that."

Bailey claimed that his business had never been so successful that he could take it for granted. "People always ask how long it takes before you think you've got it made," he said. "I don't know and don't ever expect to find out. Some outfits have branched out into clothing or gifts, paintings, and that sort of thing, but we've tried to stick with fishing. One never gets so big that there aren't hazards." Sometimes, he added in a transparent allusion to Abercrombie & Fitch, the famous

New York outfitter that had recently closed its doors, "the bigger they are, the harder they fall." Big investors occasionally cast covetous eyes on Bailey's business and tried to buy him out. Despite some financially attractive offers, he preferred answering only to himself and always refused.

By the early 1950s the shop had become successful enough for the Baileys to afford a ranch south of Livingston, in the spectacular and aptly named Paradise Valley. They eventually sold their spread to Peter Fonda, one of the first of many Hollywood expatriates to make their home in the Livingston area. In sixteen years there, Helen and Dan raised a daughter, Sue, and a son, John, who eventually entered the family business. Along with Dan, John at the time of my visit was one of three stockholders in Bailey's, the third member of the enterprise being Red Monical, a regular behind the counter who had started at the shop as a fourteen-year-old flytier decades before. John, at age thirty-four, had recently assumed direction of the shop and presidency of the corporation. "He's really running the business now," said Dan. "I'm chairman of the board and just give advice."

Clearly, he did a great deal more than that. John oversaw day-to-day operations and initiated marketing strategies like converting to a full-color catalog and expanding its distribution, but Dan remained a key ingredient in the shop's success. He was a *presence* there: whenever a customer walked into Dan Bailey's, he knew he would find . . . Dan Bailey. The shop had succeeded in no small measure as a projection of Dan's personality and a philosophy that fly-fishing isn't a discipline but a sport, and less a sport than a pastime. The 1970s had seen the emergence of "technical" fishing and the angler-entomologist as the new Brahmin of the sport, trends that Bailey quietly resisted. Charley Waterman told me of a young angler he noticed in the shop one day who, deeply into aquatic entomology, littered his talk with the Latin names of stream insects. Dan listened patiently to the young man's account of the compound hatch he'd matched on one of the local spring creeks, then responded with his own story about catching a big Yellowstone brown: "Well, I took this Muddler, and I slammed it down there about an inch-and-a-half from the bank, and I went put-put-put-put just like that and he came right out and smacked it."

In fact, Dan admitted to fishing on occasion the demanding spring creeks around Livingston, although with no pretense about matching their troublesome hatches of tiny mayflies and caddis. But his preference was always for the Yellowstone or smaller freestone streams where the particular pattern matters less than how you present it to the fish. One of his favorites was a bright Royal Wulff like the one that for years adorned the cover of the Bailey catalog. Other flies that he carried—and had originated—included the Spuddler, Maribou Muddler, and Mossback Nymph. Although his fly box held streamers and nymphs, he told me, "I do better than 95 percent of my fishing with dry flies. I'm not very good with nymphs. I never mastered them, and I'm not much of an exact imitationist, either."

After seventy years, Bailey's feeling for fly-fishing ran as deep and strong as his beloved Yellowstone, and it was a rare Sunday when he and Helen didn't head off in their Jeep camper to some secluded stream in the mountains. "We prefer places that aren't so well-known, with fewer big fish but more solitude," he said. "One of the prime ingredients of fishing to my mind is solitude, and it's almost disappeared. The only problem I have now is husbanding my strength. I used to be able to fish the Yellowstone from sunup to dark, or work all day and go fishing in the evening and then party most of the night. I've reached the point where I can't do that anymore."

On the red license folder that Bailey gave free to customers was an inscription that amounted to a personal credo: "Fish More—Live Better—Live Longer." For Dan Bailey, age and time seemed to vanish in the whisper of moving water and the expectation of a trout rising on the next cast to an artfully floated dry fly. His friend Charley Waterman recalled the many times he went fishing with Bailey and watched him disappear upstream: "He wouldn't come back to camp until some ungodly hour way past dark. I've been on innumerable search parties for Dan Bailey and driven a lot of miles looking for him, but snickering all the while. I knew what had happened—he just couldn't stop fishing—and I knew he'd be back."

The story I wrote about Dan Bailey for *Rod & Reel* appeared, more or less in the form above, later that year, about the same time as the one for *People* (rewritten by the editors to play up the celebrity angles and titled "Montana's Lord of the Flies Is Dan Bailey, Kingfish of an Angler's Paradise").

A friend of mine at *People* once made a wise observation about a journalist's pitfall he called the "false intimacy" of the interview. For better or worse, our society gives a writer license to walk into people's lives and probe them with questions that in other contexts would garner a punch in the nose. But getting to know anyone as sweet-tempered as Dan Bailey, even in such a superficial way, was a privilege, made more so by the letter I received from him not long after the article appeared. Typed by Dan on his old upright and dated January 29, 1982, it read,

> Dear Jim,
>
> Someone just gave me a copy of your article in Rod & Reel. This is great. In my opinion the best ever done of me. Now I am trying to get a few extra copies of that Nov.-Dec. issue.
>
> I hope you come back to fish with us again this summer. I am still a bit embarrassed about the

small amount of time I gave you on the stream and I would like to take more time with you when you return.

Our 1982 catalogue will be out in a few days and we are sending you a copy then.

Thanks again for all the great publicity you have given us.

Sincerely,
Dan Bailey

It was a shock to learn the following spring that Dan and his beloved Helen had recently died within a few weeks of each other.

As it happened, I heard this sad news just before departing for a trip with some alumni of Princeton University, where I worked, whom I was helping to shepherd through Peru. During the several days we spent in the Andes I was able to sneak off for a few hours' fishing on the Vilcanota, the river that flows through the Sacred Valley of the Incas. Except for the terraced slopes, stone ruins, and colorfully dressed peasants herding llamas, I might have been in Paradise Valley fishing the Yellowstone. Rummaging through my fly box, I selected an outsized Bitch Creek Special, a concoction of black and yellow chenille and rubber legs purchased the summer before at Bailey's. I had heard that Dan, not long before his death, had remarked that anyone who wished to remember him should do so by going fishing.

So it was with old Dan in mind that I pumped my rod and shot a cast into the roiling currents of the Vilcanota. A dozen casts later the line stopped short in its drift, and when I pulled up I was fast to a fish. It was not a big rainbow, only a little over twelve inches, but deep bodied and strong, and as bright as a fresh-run salmon. It would never have made the Wall of Fame, but I know Dan Bailey would have admired it.

## TWO

*Ed Van Put:
The Prince
of Gloam*

Ed Van Put's fishing outfit wasn't much to look at. As we readied for an evening on the upper Delaware River at Callicoon, New York, he slipped into boot-foot waders and a frayed fishing vest and strapped a dented aluminum fly box onto his chest. From beneath the peak of a Boston Red Sox cap he squinted at the broad river. Tucking an old fiberglass rod under his arm, he tied on a size-fourteen Adams. He was ready to go before I had finished lacing up my wading boots.

When I fished with Van Put in June 1992, he had been haunting the upper Delaware for a quarter century. During a stretch in the 1970s he fished it more than a hundred days a year. In its size and sweep the Delaware resembles a western river like the Yellowstone, and it can confound eastern anglers used to smaller streams. Those who regularly fish the Big D have long spoken in awe of Van Put's ability to consistently catch its wild rainbows.

We were after some of those rainbows now, and at Ed's suggestion I moved into the head of the run just below the Callicoon bridge while Ed took station fifty yards farther downstream. It seemed like no time before he was into a fish. Probing the riffle with a pair of nymphs, I caught and released a rainbow of thirteen inches (small by Delaware standards), then picked up an obese sucker that fought with the vigor of a waterlogged towel. Not counting the latter, we each had one fish, a parity I doubted would last.

The sun slipped behind the hills on the Pennsylvania shore and the silver current gathered the fading light, but it soon became too dark to see my fly line. Some anglers who'd been fishing above the bridge trudged back to their cars. I would have quit too but for my companion. As he put it: "When you hear the car doors slam, it's like a signal for the fish to come up."

It was the start of Ed's Hour. As the sky deepened, he ranged up and down the pool like the proverbial stalking heron, looking and listening for the occasional rise and seldom casting unless he detected one. The water wasn't exactly boiling, but Van Put is uniquely adept at spotting the fleeting rise forms of Delaware trout after dark, as if he'd been born with extra rod cells in his retinas. I was blanked for the rest of the evening, but when we left the water at 9:45 his tally included rainbows of twelve and fifteen inches and a fifteen-inch brown. It was a respectable if unexceptional showing for the man called the Admiral of the Delaware, but whom I think of as the Prince of Gloam.

I had met Van Put the day before at his house, midway between Roscoe and Livingston Manor, in the heart of New York's Catskill Mountains, where he lives at the base of a wooded ridge with his wife and their two boys, Lee (named for one of Ed's angling mentors, Lee Wulff) and John. In the backyard, between Judy Van Put's vegetable garden and the kids' upright swimming pool, were cages holding a trio of roosters—dun, red, and grizzly—raised by Ed for their hackles. The birds were descendants of ones given to him years before by another of his mentors, the late Catskill flytier Harry Darbee. (The birds that produce Metz necks also trace their ancestry to Darbee's cocks.) Van Put used to kill the birds and skin out their necks, he told me, but now just plucked a feather whenever he needed one. "I'm sure they don't like it," he said, "but it's better than dead."

Ed was in his mid-fifties and had lived in the Catskills for twenty-seven years. He worked for the New York Department of Environmental Conservation as a fisheries technician, a felicitous blending of vocation and avocation that kept him enviably in touch with the region's trout waters. His primary job was securing fishing easements from property owners, and many of the public-access points in the Catskills (including the one at Callicoon) are there because of him. On spring weekends he taught at Lee and Joan Wulff's fly-fishing school in nearby Lew Beach.

He was born and raised 150 miles, but a world away, from the upper Delaware in grimy Passaic County, New Jersey. As a kid he fished with bait on the Passaic River ("carp were our salmon") and later fly fished on lakes for bluegills and bass. His dad, a school custodian and former stevedore who had emigrated from Belgium, didn't fish at the time; in a reversal of the usual roles, Ed taught the old man to fly fish after Emil Van Put retired to the Catskills. Ed's widowed mother, Agnes, lived across the road from him on the banks of Willowemoc Creek. After high school, Ed spent two years in the army and then returned home and worked in construction. Weekends he explored the streams of the Catskills. He moved there in 1965 and through a classified ad found a clerk's job in the sporting goods section of a department store in Livingston Manor. "I worked six days a week," he recalled, "but the Willowemoc was just a few minutes away."

The Delaware wasn't much farther. Harry Darbee introduced him to the big river, and he soon made it his own. "I'd go on binges, camping out for nine days at a stretch and fishing till

10:30 every night through May and June," he said. Cold water from the bottom of dams recently completed on the Delaware's East and West Branches had turned its main stem into a superb tailwater fishery. The volume of water released was more than double what it is today. "They'd *sock* it down. In July and August you fished in long underwear but still had to get out of the water to warm up." The river's solitude pulled at him, too. "Back then, you could fit everybody who fished the Delaware into a school bus, and they were mostly bait fishermen. For days the only person I'd see was the engineer on the train." Van Put made friends with landowners and traded six-packs for access, but he failed to win over one resident misanthrope who took potshots at him on the river. "You could hear the bullets going by overhead. It was real *Deliverance* country."

The fishing made it worth the risk. On dries, Van Put has caught rainbows up to twenty-three inches and browns to twenty-four. The Delaware's rainbows, which outnumber its browns about seven to one, average sixteen inches and are strong, thick-bodied trout that run like bonefish.

Before logging in the mid-nineteenth century ravaged the river and forever changed its ecology, the upper Delaware, including its East and West Branches and its principal Catskill tributaries, the Beaverkill and Neversink, supported brook trout, the native char of eastern North America. Brown trout, imported from Germany, were first stocked in Delaware tributaries in 1887. Rainbows are native to the Pacific slope, and according to a long but now discredited legend, their Delaware lineage dated from 1895, when a wreck on the railroad that parallels the river delayed a train carrying cans of rainbow fry. Concerned that the fish would die, the brakeman—one Dan Cahill, after whom the Light Cahill is named—dumped them into Callicoon Creek. This incident may have occurred, but as Van Put learned in research on the history of upper Delaware fisheries, rainbows were stocked on its tributaries as early as 1881, just three years after eggs from rainbows were first transported from California and cultured in eastern hatcheries. The descendants of these fish moved into the Delaware, where they came to thrive under the tailwater conditions present since the 1960s.

"Delaware rainbows are genetically different, something special—a fourteen-incher can put you into backing," said Van Put. "And because it's got plenty of space and food, every fish has the potential to be twenty inches."

Anglers have discovered the main Delaware in the years since Van Put began fishing it. Although by eastern standards the river is far from crowded, on weekends its more accessible pools can be hit hard, and the river supports a small industry of guides who drift it in McKenzie boats. Van Put said he missed the solitude but appreciated that the Delaware now had friends to fight for it, and he believed that the difficulty of fishing it kept crowding in check. "It's not for the average fisherman," he said. "A guy who'll catch fifteen or twenty fish on the Beaverkill can come over here and get skunked." Van Put's meticulous angling records indicate that even he averages only about one fish per hour on the Delaware. Surveys conducted in the 1990s by New York's Department of Environmental Conservation show that the typical Delaware angler catches one fish every *five* hours.

The first problem is finding fish on a river so intimidatingly large. Long sections are deep, flatwater pools ("eddies," in local parlance). A few night-fishing specialists take lunker browns from these stretches, but otherwise they're not especially productive. Rainbows prefer the faster water between pools, but even in these "riffs" the current is often so slow that feeding trout cruise as they would in a lake rather than hold position—working their way upstream and then drifting back to their starting point and repeating. For the angler, the trick is to spot a rise, anticipate when and where the fish will rise again, and cast to that spot. The technique may be easy in principle, but mastering it is something else. It takes a practiced eye even to see the rises, which are sporadic and subtle— the current swallows them up—and the task is doubly difficult in the dusky conditions preferred by Van Put. "I catch a lot of fish in the last thirty minutes of the evening," said the Prince of Gloam. "It's not exactly night fishing, because there's still a little light. I call it 'dark' fishing. You can't see the fly anymore, but you can see rises. Cast ahead of them, and if the fish stop rising, hold your cast until they start coming up again."

A Delaware rainbow takes a dry fly deliberately, and if you see the take it's easy to strike too quickly and miss. "You've got to *strike the rise,* not the fly," declared Van Put. "Even if I can see the fly, I try not to look at it. If I have to, I'll zap my night vision with a flashlight."

This kind of fishing requires wading into position for short, controlled casts. For tackle Van Put favors a white (for visibility), six-weight, double-tapered line attached to a venerable Hardy Princess reel. His rod of choice: an eight-foot, one-piece fiberglass model, one of three custom-made for him by Vince Cummings fifteen years before. Van Put likes a one-piece because the ferrules on two-piece rods wear out after a season of intensive fishing. He believes that the softness of fiberglass makes for fewer breakoffs when striking a fish, and its slow reaction time gives the trout a split second more to chomp down on the fly. "Graphite's fine for casting," he said. "Its stiffness makes for great distance, but it's very unforgiving. I've seen people using graphite rods leave a lot of flies in fish or miss strikes because they're too quick."

For his fly, Ed prefers an Adams—in size fourteen in normal conditions, but size sixteen or eighteen in low water or if the fish are feeding on smaller stuff. Its mottled gray dressing makes this dry fly one of the great generic patterns, of course, and Van Put believes that fish can more easily spot its dark silhouette in dim light. He likes to fish it even when it is patently the "wrong" fly, for example, during a hatch of Hendriksons or Green Drakes. While Van Put is reputed to fish the Adams exclusively, a glance through his fly box belies this. If no fish are rising, he said, he may search the water with a Chuck Caddis, a Henryville Special, or a Cream Variant. For nymphs he favors the Zug Bug, and he occasionally fishes downstream with traditional wet flies like the Royal Coachman and Cow Dung.

My first chance to see Ed Van Put in action came on the Sunday I met him at his house. We drove down to the mouth of Bouchoux Brook, where a parking lot maintained by the National Park Service (the upper Delaware is a National Scenic River) offers easy access. It was midafternoon, and we began by investigating a riffle on the outside of a sweeping bend, just above where the brook enters the Delaware. A chill wind blew off the pewter river. A front was moving through, and the weather had turned unseasonably raw for June. Ed had wisely worn a thick wool sweater, but I was underdressed in a cotton shirt. I noticed some small, dark mayflies coming off despite the cold. "Looks like a Paraleps," I said, referring to a Blue-Winged Olive mayfly in the *Paraleptoplebia* genus, but Van Put didn't know and didn't care. Nor did the trout, which were nowhere in evidence, and I was skeptical when Ed said they ought to be showing at dusk: "I've seen so many rising here in that last hour that it gave me the shakes."

We moved downstream to try a fast run cutting against a rip-rap bank. Ed detected an occasional rise on the broken current. He knelt on a barely submerged rock and cast to a fish. After failing to move it, he switched to a smaller Adams and cast again, throwing slack in the line and a bit of body English for a good drift—strike!—and breaking off the fly. With a fresh fly he cast ahead of another fish. "It's right there. Take it, take it, take it . . . *Perfect!*" The Adams completed its drift unintercepted. Van Put laughed. "Geez, he came up right before the fly got to him!"

By the end of the afternoon he'd caught an eight-inch rainbow and a chub. Although his total stood at two more fish than mine, I wondered if his abilities were overrated.

My doubts vanished that evening after we moved back to fish again at the mouth of Bouchoux Brook. I staked a position opposite Ed on the New York side of the run. Following his example, I tied on an Adams and scanned the glistening flow, looking for rises but for the life of me seeing none. The cold made it hard to concentrate. I'd returned to the car to add several shirts and a windbreaker to my outfit, but every time the breeze picked up it started me shivering. My back ached, and I felt about as miserable as the pair of dying fish I noticed ghosting at my feet. They were spawned-out shad, a remnant of the great run that ascends the Delaware each spring. The three-to-five-pound shad that survive spawning become avid feeders and can be caught on dry flies, but trout chauvinist Van Put regards them as a nuisance. He can distinguish their rises—"they make a popping sound, like a bluegill"—and avoids casting to them.

I was spacing on the shad when Ed's whining reel grabbed my attention. He had a fish on, and his Hardy sang like a sewing machine at full throttle. He let the fish run—there was no other option—his bent rod silhouetted against the gray horizon and the line cutting downstream. The fish made several more runs, each shorter than the last, until angler and trout were maneuvering in a half circle defined by the radius of Ed's rod. He ended this pas de deux with a deft flick of his net, hefting a sixteen-inch rainbow.

Minutes after releasing the fish he had on another. It was getting darker fast. Bats flitted silently above the water, and Van Put began to fade like Alice's Cheshire Cat until all I could see of him was his disembodied bleached-tan vest. Yet even while he played the fish, his eyes searched for more rises. "There's one just above you, Jim!" he yelled. Of course, I couldn't see it. A bat bumped my fly line, and soon it became so dark that even the bats called it a night. When at last we reeled in, Ed had caught three rainbows, the largest eighteen inches, and a twenty-one-inch brown.

Watching Ed Van Put fish, I concluded, was like observing a world-class athlete performing in his own hyperspace. I had witnessed a crepuscular tour de force, the piscatorial equivalent of Wayne Gretzky or Larry Bird trumping the opposition. Ed's Red Sox baseball cap recalled his boyhood worship of Ted Williams, and it begged comparisons between the two. Ed brings to his angling the same intensity that Williams (no mean angler himself) applied to hitting a baseball. The Prince of Gloam and the Splendid Splinter share other attributes, among them superb vision (Van Put's is 20/15, uncorrected) and the seemingly opposite qualities of restlessness and patience. Van Put seldom stays in one spot very long yet resists the urge to cast aimlessly. Williams was perpetual motion at the plate but waited for the right pitch. Also, as Lee Wulff observed, Van Put brings to his fishing a predator's instincts. He *stalks* trout.

He exemplifies two nuggets of angling wisdom rattling around in my head. One is the late John Voelker's admonition to "hoard the cast." Another is a line from a magazine interview with Lefty Kreh: "Ninety percent of all fishing knowledge is local knowledge." To be sure, Van Put's intimacy with the Delaware gives him an incalculable advantage on that river, but his methods and especially his philosophy—that how you present a fly is more important than the fly itself—are broadly applicable to all rivers and fishing situations. Art Lee, an angling writer with whom Van Put has long maintained a friendly rivalry, jokes that Ed's hands exude a unique chemical that make his flies irresistible to fish. Van Put's near-legendary status among Delaware anglers both flatters and bemuses him. He insists that his skills are nothing special, that it is just a matter of putting in the time—a hundred days a year for twenty-five years!—and using the right techniques.

A few days later, I spent a morning fishing a nice run of pocket water upstream from Callicoon. A sparse caddis hatch brought up a few fish, and in the glare of day their rises were fairly easy to see. Doing everything Ed's Way, I landed and released a bright rainbow a hair short of sixteen inches. It was my first Delaware 'bow ever on a dry fly, and a beginning.

## THREE

# Ken Reinard: The Colonial Angler

In the summer of 1787, George Washington and his friend Gouverneur Morris took time off from the Constitutional Convention in Philadelphia for a trip to nearby Valley Forge. Their intention was to "get trout," wrote Washington in his diary, although Morris appears to have done all the fishing. While the general toured his winter encampment of nine years before, Morris ranged up and down Valley Creek, a pretty limestone stream, casting for brook trout.

Valley Creek still looks much as it did during Revolutionary times, and on a fall day in 1993, as I watched Ken Reinard probe its gentle runs with his bamboo pole, horsehair line, and antique flies, it was easy to forget that the twenty-first century was just a few years away. Reinard bills himself as the Colonial Angler, and whenever he goes a-fishing he dresses the part: buckled shoes, knickers, knee-length coat, floppy felt hat, and

Ben Franklin glasses. On this particular outing, as always, he drew plenty of double takes from joggers and other fishermen. When a gray-haired woman asked if he'd pose for a photograph with her grandson, the Colonial Angler cheerfully obliged, taking a break from what had been a fishless morning. His lack of success owed at least as much to the low water as to his vintage tackle, which limits him to short, downwind casts. Reinard works without a reel ("winches" were used in the eighteenth century, but mainly for salmon fishing), and his eight-foot line attaches directly to the rod. "It kind of handicaps you," he says. "That's one of the things that's neat about fishing this way."

The idea for the Colonial Angler had come to Reinard several years before. Since 1984 he has been a member of the German Regiment, a group of reenactors in south-central Pennsylvania who spend weekends restaging Revolutionary War battles. Whenever they bivouacked near a stream, Reinard, a lifelong fisherman, gazed at it longingly. But reenactors have to stay in character, and anyone fishing with modern tackle risked getting drummed out of the unit. So Reinard began researching early fishing methods and tackle. Before long, he was making his own rods, hooks, and flies, following instructions in classics like *A Treatise of Fishing with an Angle* (1496) and Izaak Walton's *Compleat Angler*, first published in 1653.

Since going public as the Colonial Angler in May 1991, Reinard told me, he'd used his venerable tackle to catch smallish brook and brown trout. He had played but broken off a trout of fourteen inches, and on the Yellow Breeches, one of his state's premier streams, he once raised an eighteen-inch rainbow but missed the strike. "On a short line, hooking is entirely different," he said.

The Colonial Angler claimed to have resisted the temptation to fish with what Walton and his contemporaries called "ground bait" (a.k.a. worms). One summer, fishing the pond at the Governor's Mansion in Colonial Willamsburg, Virginia, he hammered carp and bluegills with a Soldier Palmer, his favorite fly and a pattern that's been fooling fish for at least three centuries. Its secret may be in its simplicity—a bit of red wool wrapped with tinsel and palmered with rusty hackle. It looks and fishes like a Woolly Worm. But the Soldier Palmer derives from an even simpler pattern, the Red Hackle, which is basically the same fly minus the tinsel. Dame Juliana Berners, the English nun purported to have written the *Treatise* (scholars dispute the authorship of this first book in English on fishing), included something like the Red Hackle—she called it the Ruddy Fly—in her "jury" of twelve patterns. And the first known reference to fly-fishing, a third-century description of Macedonian anglers by the Roman naturalist Aelian, also mentions a fly tied with red wool and wound with rooster feathers.

Whatever the fly at the end of the line, try fishing with Reinard's gear for a minute and you'll appreciate modern tackle as never before. His ten-foot cane pole must weigh a pound—easily five times as much as a graphite rod. Still, it's dainty compared to some of the cudgels employed by early anglers. Charles Cotton, Walton's friend and coauthor of the later editions of the *Compleat Angler,* fished for trout with a rod of eighteen feet. Although the jointed rods described by Dame Juliana used crude iron or brass ferrules, by Cotton's day most rods were assembled from wooden sections that were spliced together, with the junctures secured by linen wrappings. The angler assembled his rod for the season and kept it in a streamside "long box."

The documentation on fishing in Colonial America is sketchy, especially as it pertains to tackle, but advertisements in newspapers of the era show that merchants sold rods, lines, and flies. By the 1730s, angling clubs were springing up in Philadelphia, and New York fishermen were casting flies on the streams and ponds of a Manhattan that was still mostly woods and farmland.

Often tackle was imported from England, but some must have been manufactured locally. Anglers presumably made their own equipment too, perhaps following instructions in books like Walton's and Berners's. That, at least, is the assumption on which the Colonial Angler has built his persona.

A few weeks prior to our outing on Valley Creek, I had visited Reinard at his home near Lancaster, Pennsylvania. I shouldn't have been surprised to find the Colonial Angler living in a ranch house in a subdivision. On his kitchen table he had laid out a smorgasbord of furs and feathers and an array of tools for making flies and hooks. Authenticity is a paramount concern to Reinard ("all the reenactments I've done have drummed into this Dutchman's thick head the importance of historical correctness"), and he follows the old recipes for flies as closely as possible. For now, hackle for his flies comes from garden-variety roosters like Rhode Island Reds, but as he told me at the time, he hoped to begin raising Booted Bantams and other vintage breeds common to eighteenth-century barn-yards.

Reinard's raw material for making lines is hair from a horse's tail. It must come from a stallion or a gelding, he said, because urine stains weaken the hairs from a mare's tail. He builds his lines in sections, which are looped at both ends and joined one to the other. To demonstrate, he drew three strands from a skein of hair that was indeed "the color of glass," just as Dame Juliana prescribed. The hairs are secured at one end to a board and braided, and the ends are knotted into loops. He then wraps the knots with silk thread and rubs the completed rig with wax, which enhances the hairs' natural translucence. It takes Reinard about an hour and a half to make one three-foot-long section.

The sections of line vary in width according to the number and thickness of hairs used in their construction. Reinard makes sections of three, six, nine, twelve, and eighteen hairs. He loops them together, building a tapered line that can be lengthened or shortened—right on the stream, if need be—by adding or removing sections. His flies are "snelled": they have built-in leaders, allowing them to be looped directly to the line. In his daytime job Reinard clerked in an outdoor shop (Trout Run Sports in Ephrata), so he knew his modern tackle too. He smiled at the "innovation" of loop-to-loop connectors. "Most fishermen don't realize these are nothing new."

A single horsehair has a breaking strength of about a pound, so three hairs are roughly equivalent to a leader of three-pound test. Our piscatorial ancestors went as fine as one hair, and Cotton routinely caught trout on two hairs (un-braided); anyone requiring stouter stuff, he sniffed, "deserves not the name of angler." A more prudent Berners recommended nine hairs for trout and fifteen for salmon. Reinard told me he has landed sunnies on two hairs and trout on three.

Although silk was in use for making lines by the 1680s, horsehair remained the material of choice through most of the 1700s, and woven horsehair lines persisted on some English streams into the later 1800s. Silkworm gut for snelled leaders entered the picture in the early 1700s but took a century to supplant horsehair.

For obvious reasons, not the least of which was the desire to stay out of divorce court, the Colonial Angler eschewed Berners's mandate to dye lines different colors for the seasons in which they are fished. The Dame concocted dyes from a veritable witch's brew of ingredients, including lye, alum, "juice of walnut leaves," and vitriol, a type of sulfuric acid. A "right good" brown called for soaking the hairs for two days in a mixture of "strong ale and soot." For a "tawny color," she advised, immerse them for five hours in lime water and a day in "tanner's ooze."

Making hooks, wrote Dame Juliana, "is the subtlest and hardest art," and she would get no argument from anyone who has watched Reinard make his. Each one takes him a half hour. "Berners and Walton said to start with a 'square-headed needle,' but where do you find those?" he asked. Instead, Reinard begins with sewing needles and cuts the eyes off. He took a needle and did exactly that. Then he grabbed a propane torch, lit it, and with a pair of pliers held the needle to the hissing blue flame. "This anneals the hook—it takes the temper out of it," he said. "I'll admit the torch isn't very authentic. I'm still looking for a little charcoal furnace."

After the blackened needle cooled at room temperature, it was pliable enough for Reinard to shape it on a hook bender, a block of wood with the surface partially cut away, leaving a raised template. He inserted the point of the needle into a slot in the template and bent the shaft around it. Removing the freshly formed hook, he cut the shaft to the correct length, put the blunt end into an anvil, and hammered it into a flat, triangular head to hold the snell. To give it temper, he reheated the hook and quenched it in water, removed the carbon scale with a file, heated the hook a third time until it glowed a deep indigo, then slowly quenched it in candle tallow. (Reinard deliberately left out one step: raising the barb, which is done with a chisel before the needle is bent. A barbless hook facilitates catch-and-release fishing, a concept that doubtless would have raised an eyebrow on old Ike Walton.)

A few strokes of the file sharpened the hook, and it was now ready for "arming," or snelling. Reinard pinched the hook in his fingers—he spurns a fly-tying vise, a relatively modern invention—and with silk thread secured three strands of horse's hair to the shaft. Later, after "dressing" the hook with fur and feathers, he would braid the strands and tie the ends in a loop.

On a visit to Montana I had a chance to field-test several antique fly patterns, and the experience convinced me that Berners, Cotton, and company knew what they were talking about. I had been corresponding with Reinard, and just before leaving I received in the mail a sampling of Red Hackles and Soldier Palmers he had dressed on modern hooks. I supplemented these with some flies I tied myself. They were based on a pattern in an eighteenth-century English manuscript that I found in the Kienbusch Angling Collection, a depository of rare fishing books and tackle in the library of Princeton University. The bound manuscript gave the recipes for twenty-five patterns, and the anonymous author had thoughtfully inserted into the pages a sample of every fly described. Leafing through this little book, I was struck by the naturalness of the flies, some of which resembled the modern, soft-hackle "flymph" patterns popularized by Vernon S. "Pete" Hidy in the 1940s. The blackened hooks were mostly sizes twelve and fourteen, but a few flies were tied on hooks approaching a diminutive size eighteen.

These flies, I knew, could catch fish today. The one I copied had a body of peacock herl wound with red hackle and was called the Peacock Palmer. Along with the flies Reinard had sent me, it would make for several outstanding days on my Montana trip, beginning with a morning on the Gallatin River.

I was fishing some pocket water a short walk downstream from the Williams Bridge, a few miles south of Bozeman, just off the road toward West Yellowstone. Normally I would work this kind of run with a weighted stone fly nymph, and when I tied on a Red Hackle, I did so more out of a sense of experiment than confidence. Otherwise, everything seemed right. The sun cutting through the cottonwoods flashed off the water, and the air was alive with mayfly spinners and brown caddis flies. I made a short cross-stream cast and followed the line as it sucked into the backwash of a big rock. The line surged, and to my astonishment a bright fish cleared the surface. I guided it into the shallows, slipped the barbless hook from its jaw, and released the sixteen-inch rainbow. Score one for the Colonial Angler and a fly as timeless as the river.

## FOUR

# Silas Goodrich: Fishing with the Corps of Discovery

On August 9, 1805, the thirty-three members of the Lewis and Clark expedition worked their way up the Beaverhead River in what is now southwestern Montana. Since leaving St. Louis more than a year before on their great journey of discovery, they had traveled by keelboat and dugout canoe twenty-six hundred miles up the Missouri River and its tributaries. They were now within a few days of the Continental Divide, beyond which lay the Columbia River and, they hoped, passage to the Pacific.

The country all around them was new to white men's eyes and austerely beautiful. Beyond the river's willow-fringed banks, a sagebrush plain rolled away toward distant peaks. The men were hardly in a mood to appreciate these pristine surroundings, however, for ascending the Beaverhead (named by the Shoshoni Indians for an outcrop that resembled a swimming beaver) was proving an arduous and painful business. Hauling on elk hide ropes, they strained against the thigh-deep current, slipping and cursing as they dragged their supply-laden canoes yard by painful yard up the swift mountain river.

That evening, as most of them lay exhausted near the present site of Dillon, Montana, one man slipped away from camp. Hunkering by the river's edge, he watched the fading light play on an eddy where some trout were feeding just beneath the surface, their dorsals bulging in the current. The sight of the fish made him forget his aching muscles and bruised feet. From a wooden spool carried in his knapsack he unwrapped several arm lengths of line and examined the hook tied at the end. Lashed to the shank was a strip of deer skin with the hair left on it.

Several buckshot pinched to the line gave the rig enough weight for him to cast it well into the current. He followed the lure as it swung into the feeding lane. One of the trout grabbed it, and the line surged from the spool and through his fingers as the fish made several runs before tiring. He hauled his prize flopping onto the bank. It was deep bodied and as long as his forearm, with broad silver flanks and a slash of red beneath its throat. In a dozen more casts he had nearly as many fish—a hearty supplement to tomorrow's breakfast of antelope steaks and pemmican.

Although the scene is imaginary, the fisherman—Silas Goodrich—was real. He was the angler of the Lewis and Clark expedition and the first non-Indian ever to fish in the Rocky Mountains. Might he have also been the first to fish the Rockies with an artificial lure? It was a question I pondered on a cloudless Montana day in July 1988, 183 years after Goodrich and the Corps of Discovery passed this way, while floating the Beaverhead in a neoprene raft, fishing for the river's celebrated trout while chasing the ghost of old Silas.

Goodrich was one of the more obscure members of the Corps of Discovery, and his biography barely fleshes out a paragraph. Born in Massachusetts, he was probably a regular soldier in his early twenties, a transfer from some other army unit in 1803 when recruited by Lewis and Clark for their epic journey across the continent. On the expedition's return from the Pacific three years later he reenlisted, but after that his name vanishes from the record. According to William Clark, he was dead by the mid-1820s.

Most of what we know about Silas Goodrich has to do with his particular obsession. As Meriwether Lewis noted in his journal, Goodrich was "remarkably fond of fishing" and routinely provided the explorers with trout and other finny fare to leaven their usual menu of deer, elk, and buffalo. It was Goodrich, Lewis recorded on June 13, 1805, who at the Great Falls of the Missouri caught "half a douzen very fine trout," between sixteen and twenty-three inches long and with a "small dash of red" under their jaws—the first record of cutthroat trout, later assigned the scientific name *Salmo clarkii* after the corps's coleader.

Goodrich also caught sauger (a first cousin to walleye) and goldeye (a panfish bearing a superficial resemblance to herring) near Great Falls, and earlier in the expedition his bag included blue and channel catfish, landed above the mouth of the Platte River in present-day Nebraska; Clark noted the fish were "verry fat" and named their camp after them. All these fish were new to science, as were seven other species recorded by Lewis and Clark on the journey: mountain sucker, steelhead (the sea-run rainbow trout of the Pacific Northwest), northern squawfish, Columbia River chub, candlefish, white sturgeon, and starry flounder. While descending the Columbia, they also observed huge runs of salmon. To a modern-day angler, the most striking omission from the Lewis and Clark list is the Rocky Mountain whitefish, which in many of Montana's streams outnumber trout by three to one. It's possible that whitefish—regarded with disdain by most trout fishermen—were far less common when western rivers were pristine.

His angling prowess aside, Goodrich seems to have been a competent but unexceptional member of the corps. I imagine him as taciturn, respected and liked well enough by the other men but keeping his own company. Fishing, apparently, was not his only diversion, for he was one of two men whom Lewis mentioned by name as contracting venereal disease from Indian women.

"Mend your line—we're coming through a good run, and I know there's a fish hogging down there," said Tim Tollett, the guide for my day's fishing on the Beaverhead and the owner of Frontier Anglers, a Dillon fly shop. Tollett (pictured, p. 45) worked the oars of the raft while I cast from the bow. I banished Silas Goodrich from my thoughts for the time being and turned my attention to fishing.

The river flowed swift and clear, its banks lined with dense willows and punctuated by thick piles of driftwood— "junk piles," Tollett called them, an ideal cover for big trout. The cold, nutrient-rich waters of the upper Beaverhead issue from the bottom of Clark Canyon Dam and are chiefly responsible for the river's dense population of large trout, many in excess of twenty inches. Named for William Clark, the dam was completed in 1964 and covers the site of Camp Fortunate, where Lewis and Clark cached their canoes prior to crossing the Continental Divide at nearby Lemhi Pass. The dam supplies the river's upper fifteen miles with a steady flow throughout the summer. The Beaverhead today may offer better fishing than it did when Silas Goodrich passed this way, although the native cutthroat have been mostly replaced by brown and rainbow trout (introduced in the late nineteenth century from Europe and California, respectively). Said Tim, "The biggest brown I've seen taken from the river was sixteen and a half pounds and the biggest rainbow fifteen."

The prospect of hooking into a lunker didn't displease me. Although I didn't mention it to Tollett, in eighteen years of fly fishing I had yet to catch a trout bigger than seventeen inches.

As we turned another bend in the river, I dropped my flies over the light-colored slope of a gravel bar. "The big browns like that blond water. They blend right into it—gives them a feeling of security," said Tollett, bearing on the oars. "Mend your line and keep those nymphs deep." I was fishing a pair of size-fourteen nymphs, a stone fly pattern, and a Pheasant Tail.

I wondered what Silas Goodrich would have thought of my flies and graphite rod. My fantasies about the deer-hair fly aside, he probably fished exclusively with bait. I assume too that he employed a hand line rather than a long, jointed rod of the type common to his era, although it's conceivable that he might have fashioned a simple pole from a willow branch. While outfitting for the expedition in Philadelphia, Lewis had purchased from George R. Lawton, the proprietor of the Old Experienced Tackle Shop, a supply of fish hooks, ten pounds of line, and what the bill of sale referred to as an "8 stave reel."[1] Common to its era, a stave reel was a spool made of two wooden discs joined at their rims by staves, or dowels. It spun around a central pillar attached to a handle. Essentially, it was a device for storing a hand line. Goodrich might have used this reel or perhaps he carried his own tackle—the record doesn't state. Nor do the journals kept by Lewis and Clark tell us much about fishing methods. In one entry, Lewis wrote that one evening on the Missouri he "caught upward of a douzen" fish in a few minutes, using cuts of deer spleen supplied by Goodrich. The men sometimes "gigged" salmon and steelhead, although it's not clear whether this entailed snagging or spearing, and on at least one occasion a member of the party *shot* a salmon in shallow water.

Tollett maneuvered the raft into the bank to inspect a backwater he thought might hold fish. "I'm just gonna have a little peek over here," he said. "Yep—we've got two nice

---

1. For information pertaining to the "8 stave reel" I am indebted to "Incompleat Anglers on the Lewis and Clark Expedition," an article by Robert R. Hunt in the February 1997 *We Proceeded On,* the journal of the Lewis and Clark Trail Heritage Foundation.

rainbows, both of them over five pounds." I waded up carefully, keeping in the shadows of the willows, when out in the main channel a huge fish exploded. The rainbow's dark form hung over the water for what seemed an eternity before plunging back into the rushing current.

It was my first, unnerving glimpse of a Beaverhead trout. "Good God!"

The rainbows we were stalking in the backwater were just as large. Sensing our presence, one of the fish moved into deeper water before I could spot it. But the other continued feeding, floating lazily in the current as it picked off mayfly nymphs drifting just below the surface. On Tollett's instructions but without much confidence, I flipped a cast above the fish.

"Strike!" he said.

To my astonishment, the fish was on. It thrashed angrily and moved into the big water, stripping line as it took off downstream.

"Get in the boat and we'll follow!"

I slipped butt first into the bow, and we were on our way. After a hundred yards or so I had regained most of my line. We beached the raft on the opposite bank with the idea of landing the fish in the shallows. I continued taking in line until the rainbow was in a foot of water and about ten feet away. Then the line went limp.

"That happens a lot when you get them in close like that—the angle's bad, and sometimes the fly pulls loose," Tollett said.

I was disappointed, but it was not yet noon and we had most of the day still ahead of us. Back in the raft and drift fishing again, I sensed a tug and set the hook. Another fish. It felt moderately heavy, but it fought with all the vigor of a clump of moss, and its silver form slid easily to the boat.

"A whitefish," said Tollett.

I unhooked the fly from the suckerlike mouth. It plopped back into the river and instantly sank from sight.

"This river's got lots of whiteys," said Tollett. "Sometimes you'll see four or five of them lined up and feeding in a side channel, and there'll be one big rainbow right in the middle of them. The trick is to spot the rainbow and cast directly to him."

I worried that such precision casting and the ability to see fish deep in the swift current were beyond me. When we parked the raft on another gravel bar, Tollett took me to a side channel and with his X-ray vision located two fish feeding behind a junk pile. "You've got a twenty-inch brown right there and a twenty-two-inch rainbow just above him." With the help of Polaroid sunglasses I could barely make out the undulant ghosts. They could as easily have been waving grass. The fish were too deep for a drag-free drift, and after my casting put them down we moved on.

Our next stop was on the lee side of an island that split the river. The channel was shallow, and on the edge of a riffle Tollett sighted a pod of gorging fish. I pretended to see them. Following his instructions to the letter, I cast directly upstream, trying to place the leader just to the shallow side of the fish and to drive the flies deep with a tuck cast. The wind had begun blowing a gale, and I was casting right into it.

"Whoops—you just lined one of them. He's spooked."

I rested the fish for a minute and tried again. As the leader drifted back toward me I saw it pause, and struck. A flash on the bottom and the surge of the line through my fingers left no doubt. Golden in the sunlight, a heavy brown leaped, then charged downstream with me splashing in pursuit.

"I don't have a lot of experience playing and landing big fish," I said, as if it weren't obvious.

"Keep your rod high! Play him from the butt—not the tip!" Tollett coached.

The brown took me through some fast water, then paused in a side pocket. Through the taut line I could feel the sulking brute trying to shake the fly free. I prayed my tippet would hold.

"Don't let him rest. He's regaining his strength. There he goes again."

I let the fish run. By now we had invaded the territory of another angler who'd been fishing downstream of us. He reeled in his line to watch the circus. Noticing that he had a net—we had left ours in the raft—I broached the idea that perhaps he would lend it to us.

"Happy to," he said. "This is the most excitement I've had all day."

Tim took the net, and after several attempts I managed to maneuver the fish into position for him to land it. I collapsed in the shallows, holding the net half submerged while admiring the big male brown that was still so full of life. Before releasing the fish, we measured him. He was twenty inches and change, and with his deep body he may have gone four pounds. So I like to think, anyway. Just average for anyone who fishes the upper Beaverhead regularly, but for me a quantum leap in my angling experience.

The next evening I fished a tributary to the Beaverhead, a pretty spring creek on the edge of Dillon called Poindexter Slough. Its weedy currents hold a dense population of scrappy trout, most between ten and fourteen inches—my comfort zone. I walked downstream to a section I liked not far from the river. I was thinking again of Silas Goodrich. Perhaps he had waded up Poindexter to fish this very stretch.

For the first hour not much happened, but as dusk descended I noticed a swarm of mayfly spinners over the stream. They were soon falling on its slick currents, triggering a rise of trout. I hooked and released several fish on a hair-thin 7X tippet—too light to horse even small trout like these. The last fish took me bouncing downstream through the thick weed beds. By now it was nearly dark. A sliver of moon hung on the red horizon over the Bitterroot Mountains, and the spinners danced against the deepening sky.

As I released the little brown I could hear, all around me, the trout still slurping. I might have fished longer but chose instead to preserve the moment. The gathering night erased any signs of the twentieth century. It was easy to conjure a buckskinned angler tending a hand line, crouched by the bank at a downstream bend.

## FIVE

*Fran Betters:
Gentle Gnome
of the Ausable*

The West Branch of the Ausable cuts through the ancient granite of New York's Adirondack Mountains, coursing forty-five miles from its origins on the slopes of Algonquin Peak to its junction with the East Branch (in angling terms, its poor cousin) at Ausable Forks. It is a river of changing moods. Its tumbling brook trout headwaters yield to gentle flats below the Olympic ski jumps at Lake Placid. At the foot of Whiteface Mountain it becomes a canyon river, charging through flumes and gorges before a dam at Wilmington checks its flow. Below the dam it assumes once more its dominant character—a brawling, boulder-pocked river that dares an angler to wade it.

With its rough waters and giant rocks, the Ausable seems like a western river out of place. Indeed, the methods adapted to fishing it—weighted nymphs and streamers and big, bushy dry flies—are the same tactics one might use on the Big Hole or the Gunnison. Its many rocks make the Ausable, above all else, a classic pocket-water stream. Anglers who fish it successfully often do so by picking those pockets with the buoyant dry flies of Francis Betters, who since the 1960s has presided over the river from his Wilmington fly shop.

I met Betters in the summer of 1983 when John Merwin, the founding editor of *Rod & Reel* magazine (later *Fly Rod & Reel*), asked me to profile him. When I called Betters, he was noncommittal but said I could find him in the shop most anytime from eight in the morning until nine or ten at night. (He does most of his fishing, I learned later, in September and October after the tourists depart.) Tucked away amid the weeds and pines lining Route 86, the Adirondack Sport Shop—"Home of the Ausable Wulff, F. E. Betters, Prop.," as the sign announced—suggested the kind of no-frills functionalism for which Betters's flies are noted. The sole decorative element on the shop's cinder block exterior was a plywood mural depicting a skimpily clad lady angler whose fly, caught in her skirt, exposed a well-endowed derrière. The inside of the shop was cluttered even by the standards of tackle merchants—rods, nets, fly-tying materials, rain gear, boots, camping equipment, and a rack of musty paperbacks. The centerpiece was an Adirondack guide boat suspended from the ceiling and draped with a polar bear skin. "I had a guy who offered me $1,500 for that skin," Betters said. "I could have sold it three times last year, but it's not really for sale."

The shop's bespectacled proprietor had a round, boyish face that appeared younger than his fifty-odd years. Wearing a brown toupee and a flowered shirt with a string tie, he hunched at his fly-tying vise behind a counter of books and flies, opposite a portable television tuned to a soap opera. In a typical day, Betters told me, he cranked out as many as twelve dozen Ausable Wulffs, Haystacks, and Phillips Usuals. These are the dry flies that Fran Betters created for the river he has fished since the 1930s.

The relationship between Betters and the West Branch of the Ausable is almost proprietary. In the annals of fly-fishing, few men are so closely associated with a particular stream. One thinks, offhand, of Dan Bailey and the Yellowstone or Vince Marinaro and the Letort. Betters was born in Wilmington, only a stone's throw from the river, and began fishing it as a small boy under the tutelage of his father. Vic Betters was an Adirondack hunting and fishing guide and renowned as one of the best fishermen on the Ausable. His son's first trout were caught on worms in tributary creeks, but it wasn't long before he was fishing with flies on the big river. At age seven, plunking a weighted bucktail in the Flume Pool, he hooked and, with his father's help, landed a brown trout that went better than nineteen inches. A few years ago, Betters recalled, he had taken a twenty-seven-inch brown from the same pool on a weighted Hornberg, a venerable streamer pattern. "I cheated a little on that one," he said with a puckish smile. "The water was too high for dries."

Growing up, Betters fished the West Branch almost daily in season, building on the early lessons in stream craft provided by his father. In time he may have learned the river better than any man who has ever fished it. If you asked him to do so, he could probably draw from memory a map of every boulder between Wilmington Notch and Ausable Forks capable of sheltering a brown trout sixteen inches or bigger. Betters perfected the taking of these lunkers on dry flies, in particular the Ausable Wulff. "I'll fish nymphs if the trout aren't hitting dries, but I really don't like fishing streamers if I can avoid them," he said. "My father, though, was a master with big bucktails, and every year while fishing them he'd take three or four trout in the four-to-six-pound class from the Flume Pool. He was not a fly-fishing snob, however—he had a reputation as one of the better bait fishermen in the area. He'd fish minnows in the spring until the hatches started coming off, then he would switch and use nothing but flies for the rest of the season."

Ray Bergman of *Outdoor Life,* perhaps the country's most popular fishing writer of the 1930s and 1940s, was a regular on the Ausable, and he fished it often with Vic Betters. Bergman taught the rudiments of fly tying to Vic's son, who was soon experimenting with his own patterns. In 1949, as a senior in high school, Fran developed the Haystack, a highly impressionistic concoction of deer hair and dubbed fur. Nearly unsinkable when dressed with fly dope, the Haystack became a popular rough-water fly. It can be fished drag-free or skittered across the top or even popped like a bass bug. Betters tied it in four basic colors—cream, blue dun, brown, and dark gray—and in a range of sizes. Properly fished, it imitates nearly every major mayfly and caddis hatch on the Ausable. It also became the prototype of the versatile Comparadun, created by Al Caucci and Bob Nastasi in the early 1970s. The Phillips Usual, another Betters pattern, is similar to the Haystack but tied with the wiry, waterproof fur of a snowshoe hare's paw.

After a stint in the air force, three years of college, and a newspaper job in New Jersey, Betters moved back permanently to Wilmington, where he set up his fly shop in 1964. A systematic study of the river's rich insect fauna led to the Ausable Wulff, a fly that in Betters's view mimics many of the stream's larger insects. He ties his Wulff with a woodchuck tail, opossum body, impala wings, and an Adams-like hackle of brown and grizzly. The tying thread is fluorescent orange, which shows through the dubbed body and is conspicuous in the head. To human eyes, it looks at first glance like nothing in nature, although in its general color and configuration it might pass (in a trout's-eye view on broken water, at least) for an adult of one of the big stone flies that abound on the Ausable. Betters told Art Lee of *Fly Fisherman* magazine that the pattern works because he barks when lacquering the heads. Whatever the reason, the Ausable Wulff's record speaks for itself: over the years, Betters told me, he had caught with it a pair of twenty-one-and-a-half-inch browns (both in the same night) and an Atlantic salmon of over twenty pounds. Although dry flies are not associated with salt water, Betters also said that in the Florida Keys he had used it to catch king mackerel, jack crevalle, and a thirty-eight-pound tarpon.

Given that kind of success, I could understand Betters's preference for flies, and I was surprised to see a truck emblazoned with the words "Worm Warehouse" pull up to his shop. When the driver entered, Betters told him, "Give me seventy-five." He kept a supply of night crawlers on hand, he explained, to sell to "the tourists" and local bait fishermen. But to such apostates he also preached the gospel of flies. "I figure I convert fifty to seventy-five people a year from bait to flies," he boasted. "I run specials on fly tackle outfits early in the season, when the fishing is relatively easy. They'll catch a few fish on flies and get hooked themselves. A lot of those I've changed have become your typical fly-fishing snobs—they'd never go back to bait.

"Of course," he added, "most good fly fishermen start out fishing with bait anyway—it's the foundation for so much, especially nymphing. But I honestly believe there's not an instance when you can't catch more fish on flies than on bait, even in high water. I've caught big trout on dry flies when you couldn't see three inches into the water, it was so muddy. If dries aren't working, then you can go to nymphs or streamers. High water can be an easy time to catch big fish because it forces them out of their regular hiding places in midcurrent into backwashes and the tails of pools. That's why novices will sometimes catch big trout under these conditions."

Betters had refined the techniques of pocket-water fishing to match the rough-and-tumble character of the West Branch. His methods for hunting big trout place a premium on reading water and covering the stream efficiently with short, upstream casts around boulders. He emphasized that to catch large trout the angler must go after them specifically. "It's a truism that 10 percent of the fishermen catch 90 percent of the fish—and I further believe that 1 percent of those fishermen catch 90 percent of the big fish. I can think of a half dozen fishermen who consistently take large trout on this river, and they do it almost exclusively with big Ausable Wulffs—sizes eight and ten. They stay on the stream until dark or a half hour past dark, after the big fish come out of their hiding places and start feeding.

"If you want to catch big fish, it's important to pick a section of stream and really learn it. Most fishermen make the mistake of coming into an area and wandering all over the place, fishing too much water rather than concentrating on one stretch of a few hundred yards."

Reading water and evaluating the conditions, he added, are critical to locating big fish. Look for a convergence of feeding lanes (marked by gunk lines) around a particular boulder. "If the stream is low, the fish will probably be lying at the head of a boulder. If the water is high—in spring or after a heavy rain—he'll probably be lying behind it." Certain boulders in the Ausable, said Betters, can consistently yield browns of three or more pounds. "I've hooked into big fish and followed them down river three hundred yards before they broke off. Two days later, that same fish will be back under the same boulder. Last season, I caught and released a nineteen-inch brown five times—in the same spot, using the same fly, and he would always come out and take it in exactly the same way. He was under a boulder in the middle of the river, behind a place we call the Old Dump Site." After Betters related this tale of the gullible trout to a friend, the guy caught and killed it. "I told him it was all right to do that."

Later we went down to the river so that Betters could demonstrate a few of his techniques. We parked at a spot on the trophy-trout stretch known as the Shadow Rock Pool. Because it was summer and the water was low, Betters fished fine and far off. Wading into the calf-deep current, he began casting from a good seventy feet away, laying a nice, slack leader at the head of a narrow feeding lane running past a house-sized boulder on the far bank. Fishing a size-ten Ausable Wulff on a 6X tippet (much finer than I would have expected for so large a fly), he worked the lane carefully and within a half dozen casts was fast to a brightly spotted, twelve-inch-brown, a remarkable feat, considering that it was midafternoon on a warm August day in the middle of a dry spell and that he was fishing on the most heavily pounded section of the river.

When the river is running at normal height, Betters's methods challenge an angler in the most physical way. The Ausable's obstacle course of boulders and jagged bedrock makes for treacherous wading, and even in low water there are sections difficult to negotiate without a wading staff. Fran Betters's river skills seem all the more admirable given that he walks with a pronounced limp as a result of a near-fatal automobile accident in his youth. He spent two years in a hospital recuperating from a broken back and neck, and doctors told him that he might never walk again. But they hadn't counted on their patient's will or his obsession with the Ausable. After a long period of therapy, he was fishing the river again—wading its swift currents first on a pair of crutches, then on one crutch, then supported by a cane.

Although making it difficult to wade, the varied bottom of the West Branch is a prime reason for its productivity. When I called Larry Strait, a state fisheries biologist, to learn more about the river, he cited its "very good substrate," which greatly increases the amount of living area for aquatic insects. At least in its upper section, the river may also benefit from Lake Placid's sewage-treatment plant, whose discharge sweetens the water's natural acidity. The West Branch boasts what must be the densest concentration of *Acroneuria* stone flies of any stream east of the Rockies. Heavy caddis hatches come off routinely on summer mornings, and the seasonal succession of mayflies includes the Hendrickson, Gray Fox, Light Cahill, March Brown, Blue-Winged Olive, Green Drake (*Ephemera guttulata*), and September's glory, the Slate Drake, or *Isonychia*. On the upper part of the river, below the ski jumps, the Ausable Flats offer a wonderfully consistent Trico hatch from August into October.

The Green Drake hatch is surprisingly good considering that this large mayfly is associated with soft-bottom habitat. It begins coming off in mid- to late June at Ausable Forks and works its way up river about a thousand feet a day, said Betters. "We have records for the start of the hatch for the last thirty years, and the curious thing is that it's gotten later and later over that period—it used to start around the fifth of June and now it's more like the twentieth. The other odd phenomenon is that the Hendrickson hatch has gotten earlier. It used to begin about the twentieth of May and now starts around the fifth. I've talked to the biologists about this, but they say you'd have to study the river a thousand years to know why."

The West Branch is stocked heavily. In the 1980s the state was placing 45,000 browns and rainbows a year into the twenty-five-mile stretch between Lake Placid and Ausable Forks. Arguably, the West Branch was overstocked, since it has good reproduction in both the main river and its many cold-water tributaries. Betters said that he favored the heavy stocking because most of it occurred in the more accessible stretches, leaving the remoter parts to serious fishermen.

Even the popular stretches of the West Branch are lightly fished by the standards of other prime eastern streams, which Betters asserted were not in the same league with his river. "I wouldn't even compare the Ausable with the Beaverkill. And there are probably more trout in a half mile of this river than in five miles of the Battenkill. There's a three- or four-pound trout for every hundred yards—no, make that every hundred *feet*—of this river, and in the first hundred yards below the Wilmington dam I bet there are a dozen trout over three pounds."

A qualification is in order. Though a mere "tourist" fisherman of the sort that Betters dismisses, I have fished his river enough to form my own opinions. The West Branch of the Ausable is a good river, maybe even a great one, and in remoter stretches like the Bush Country, above Ausable Forks, a competent angler on a half day's outing can hook into twenty or more fish, most of them medium-sized browns or rainbows up to fourteen inches. But the river does not easily yield up the big browns for which it is noted. As Betters emphasized, you have to hunt for them, generally at dusk or after dark, and the angler who prefers action over lunkers can fish the river happily for years without seeing a trout bigger than fifteen inches. Any fish larger than that will almost surely be a brown; the rainbows, Betters assumed, either don't live to grow to that size or run down river to Lake Champlain.

Whether it's size or numbers that appeal, once an angler gets to know the West Branch, it doesn't disappoint. It is a river, wrote Ray Bergman, that "commands your respect. It tests your skill and ingenuity. It is not a stream that will appeal to the timid, the weak, or the old." For these reasons and more, I found it easy to forgive Fran Betters his Ausable chauvinism.

## SIX

# Chuck Fothergill of the Frying Pan

When I met Chuck Fothergill in 1984, he spoke of the rivers near Aspen, Colorado, with an affection born of long familiarity. He had been fishing the Frying Pan and the Roaring Fork for more than twenty years and knew these waters as well as any man. As a guide, a former tackle shop owner, the designer and distributor of his own line of fishing vests, and the author of several Rocky Mountain angling guides, he seemed in the enviable position of earning a living from the sport he loved in an area of the Rockies boasting two of the West's finest trout streams. "I can't believe," he said, "that I am so lucky."

Spawned in the alpine country of the Sawatch Range on the Continental Divide, the Roaring Fork and its major tributary, the Frying Pan, course westward toward their confluence at the resort town of Basalt, Colorado. The main stem of the Roaring Fork continues another twenty-four miles before joining the Colorado River at Glenwood Springs. The Roaring Fork offers forty miles of outstanding rainbow and brown trout fishing, with special regulations governing some of the more fertile sections near Aspen and along the lower river. The Frying Pan is a tailwater fishery, of which a fourteen-mile stretch below Reudi Reservoir is designated Gold Medal waters by the Colorado Division of Wildlife.

A stocky man with a ruddy complexion and the build of a linebacker, Fothergill looked a decade younger than his fifty years. Twice divorced, with five children ranging from their teens to early twenties, he was living at the time with a girlfriend in a trailer in Basalt, an unpretentious place whose board sidewalks and false-front buildings recalled its nineteenth-century beginnings as a railroad town on the Colorado Midland line. (The town has since been gentrified and its outskirts despoiled by monster vacation homes.) The Roaring Fork flowed, literally, through his backyard, and he could be on that water or on the Frying Pan within a minute or two of pulling on his waders. Yet like many people whose business is fly-fishing, he fished less often than might be expected. It was early August, and so far that season he had been on the river a total of two days for his own pleasure. "I've been fishing this water for a long time, and I love it as much as I ever did. But I don't have to go out and fish from dawn to dusk anymore. I can get the same pleasure out of one hour of fishing as I used to get in eight."

This was my first visit to the Aspen area, and it provided Fothergill with an excuse to treat himself to a third day of fishing as he showed me some of his favorite sections of the Frying Pan. I'd come from New Jersey primarily to fish the Roaring Fork, having heard extraordinary tales about its quality from my friend Rubby Sherr, a retired Princeton University physicist who spent many summers in Aspen. Rubby, who was past the age of chasing big trout up and down a stream, had told me of hooking, playing, and then deliberately breaking off Roaring Fork fish of awesome proportions. After listening for years to what he called his "Moby Trout" stories, it was time to verify them for myself.

The Roaring Fork, alas, refused to cooperate with my plans. Although it was midsummer, the river raged in a springlike torrent due to a late runoff of snowmelt and excessive July rains. The only alternative was the gentler Frying Pan, whose flow is tempered by the Reudi Dam.

It was a choice, in fact, that we might have made even if both streams had been fishable. As the founder and until recently the owner of Aspen's premier fly shop, Fothergill was closely identified with the rough-and-tumble Roaring Fork, a classic pocket-water stream ideally suited to the upstream, short-line, weighted-leader nymphing techniques that he had developed and promoted over the years. Although Fothergill regarded the two rivers equally highly ("I consider them the best rivers in Colorado," he stated flatly), fisheries biologists rate the

Frying Pan, which suffers less from runoff and whose fertility is enriched by its gypsum (hence alkaline) substrate, as the more productive stream. Electroshocking of the Frying Pan revealed average rainbow and brown trout populations of about four hundred fish per acre—working out, according to my calculations, to upward of seventy-five fish per hundred feet of stream. The Roaring Fork matches this in its most fertile sections but is somewhat less productive overall due to bottom scouring. Fothergill said that in early June, during the height of the runoff, he lay in bed at night and listened to the muffled thunder of boulders booming downstream. "In the eighteen miles between Aspen and Basalt the river drops more than the entire Mississippi—it's not called the Roaring Fork for nothing."

After breakfast at the Two Rivers Café in Basalt we drove up the Frying Pan toward the "quality water," as fly fishermen refer to the catch-and-release section extending for two miles below Reudi Dam. It was a perfect morning, with the valley's cottonwoods and red sandstone cliffs set off against a deep western sky. I had some familiarity with the water, having fished it by myself the previous two days. Although my success had been limited—a total of eight trout in as many hours of fishing—I'd been impressed by the many insects on the water (several types of caddis flies and mayflies, including a western Green Drake that came off throughout the day) and by the numbers of rising fish. I was looking forward to improving my score under Fothergill's guidance.

Chuck Fothergill grew up near Chicago, studied business at Baker University in Kansas, and came to Colorado in 1956. "I knew—when I was nine years old and my parents brought me here on vacation—that one day I'd live in Colorado," he recalled as we wound up the narrow road hugging the river. He had been an obsessive angler since boyhood, initially with bait and then exclusively with flies, after landing his first trout (an eight-inch brookie) on an artificial in Wisconsin at age fifteen. After college and a stint in the army, he moved to Denver to work in its burgeoning aerospace industry.

During eight years in Denver, Fothergill found his free time increasingly consumed by fly-fishing. When an opportunity arose to run the tackle department of an Aspen clothing store, he chucked his job as a personnel manager for Martin Marietta. That first fling with the tackle business quickly fizzled, but he soon found other work in Aspen, first with a ski developer, then as the manager of the town's new sewer facilities. "In the meantime," he said, "I was doing more and more fishing, and guiding on the side. It finally got to the point where I realized, 'Hey, I'm giving so much advice on fishing that I might as well make a living from it.'" In 1970 he and a friend opened Chuck Fothergill's Outdoor Sportsman, a shop specializing in fly-fishing, backpacking, and cross-country ski-ing. Tired of the demands on his time and looking for new challenges, Fothergill sold the shop in 1981.

Fothergill's latest venture was the *Colorado Angling Guide,* a spiral-bound book coauthored with Bob Sterling, an Aspen painter and architect. They later produced similar guides to Wyoming and Montana; all three are distinguished by the quality of their fold-out maps of major rivers and streams. Fothergill had also started a company specializing in fly-fishing gear. Its first product was a fishing vest incorporat-ing several novel features, including a knit collar for reducing strain around the neck and a built-in tote bag into which the entire vest could be folded for carrying or storage. The vests, whose collar design came to be widely copied, were sold through tackle stores or by mail from Fothergill's one-room of-fice near the Aspen airport. As I learned when we stopped there for a brief visit, the man who gave his name to Fothergill Designs, Inc., functioned as CEO, financial officer, marketing director, secretary, and gofer. The receptionist was a telephone answering machine.

As a man dependent for his living on rivers, Fothergill stressed the importance of conservation. With his friend Georges Odier, a former director of the Aspen Chamber of Commerce and a past president of the local chapter of Trout Unlimited, he was instrumental in establishing the town's sani-tation system in the mid-1960s. As a result of their efforts, the

Roaring Fork runs clear and clean even at the height of the ski season. Fothergill also credited enlightened fisheries management for preserving quality fishing around Aspen and in other parts of Colorado. He noted that the seven miles of the Roaring Fork below Aspen have benefited from special regulations for more than twenty years. The Frying Pan had come under similar restrictions in the late 1970s, as had many more of the state's best waters. For too long, said Fothergill, Colorado had lagged behind more conservation-minded Montana in implementing catch-and-release, although it had lately made up for lost time.

The need for such controls on the best Colorado waters became apparent as we proceeded up the Frying Pan and past Seven Castles Pool, named for the sandstone battlements that overlook it. Every good run was occupied by at least one fisherman and sometimes by three or four. I was used to this kind of pressure on eastern waters but found it discouraging to see such crowding in the West. Part of the problem was the high water on the Roaring Fork, which had pushed anglers onto the Frying Pan; it was also a weekend in the middle of tourist season. But the real culprit was demographics—Colorado is a highly urbanized state whose citizens love the outdoors. As state fisheries biologist Barry Nehring later told me, "We're selling 800,000 fishing licenses a year in Colorado. There are more fishermen here than in Utah, Montana, and Wyoming combined. Our division is very much into the business of people management."

Despite the crowding, we managed to find several good sections without fishermen. Fothergill pulled off the road, and we hustled into our gear. "I'm looking for the drakes but don't see them yet," he said.

When the first stretch failed to produce, we drove upriver another half mile and stopped at a vacant run near the head of a long pool. It was close to 11 A.M. now, and the first of the Western Green Drakes began to show—big slate duns fluttering over the water or riding precariously on the swift current.

Fothergill had tied up some large (size 10) dry flies in a drake pattern but chose instead to fish the start of the hatch with an olive nymph. Using a floating line with a leader weighted with several twisted-on lead strips, he quartered a short cast upstream. He held the rod tip high, his arm angled like the Statue of Liberty's, and kept it that way through most of the drift. As the line drew abreast of him and continued downstream, he followed it with the rod, which he lowered gently to maintain a drag-free float. At the end of the drift he lifted the rod, swinging the nymph toward the surface. Probing the run carefully, he was quickly into a fat rainbow, which leaped explosively and stripped line off the reel as it charged downstream. Within the next ten minutes he caught and released several more rainbows between thirteen and fifteen inches.

I had witnessed a bravura demonstration of the "outrigger" technique developed by Fothergill and named by his friend Lefty Kreh, who borrowed the term from ocean fishing. On a deep-water fishing boat, an outrigger holds the line high off the surface while trolling. In the Fothergill method, the high rod cuts down on drag by minimizing the amount of line on the water.

As more Green Drakes appeared, we began to see rising fish. Soon dry flies were working for us, and before the day was over we'd happily lost count of all the fish—mainly rainbows but with a few browns and one rare brook trout—caught on a variety of dries and nymphs. We spent a blissful half hour in a side channel, casting directly upstream and hooking into fish after fish. What impressed me most was the strength of Frying Pan trout, for they were almost all heavy, deep-bodied fish that fought with fury. As we drove back along the stream, it seemed that every pool had at least one angler struggling, rod bent, with a fish on his line. Fothergill marveled at the sight: "Will you look at that—just everybody's catching fish. It's really a wonderful thing to see."

The richness of the Frying Pan is celebrated in the works of one of Fothergill's friends, angler-entomologist Ernest Schwiebert, who in the early 1950s did research for his book *Matching the Hatch* on the Pan's Reudi stretch, an especially fertile section that was later inundated by the Reudi Reservoir. "Every time I fish the Frying Pan," wrote Schwiebert, "I fully expect that wonderful stream to serve up some species that is completely foreign to me."

Although damming the river destroyed several miles of prime meadow habitat, it also benefited the fishery in important ways. The Reudi Dam moderates runoff, making the Frying Pan fishable (in most years) at least a month earlier than the Roaring Fork. And because water is released from the bottom of the dam, the river remains cool in summer (with water temperatures in the low fifties) and ice-free in winter. The dam's negative effects, biologist Barry Nehring told me, included some reduction in the rate of fish growth due to the colder average temperature; the dam also prevents rainbows from reproducing in the first three or four miles below it because the water released during the spring spawning season is too cold to incubate eggs. Consequently, the Division of Wildlife maintained this part of the fishery by stocking fingerlings.

Fothergill thought too that the Reudi Dam may have reduced the population of big stone flies (*Pteronarchys californica*—the famed "salmon fly" of Montana waters) on the upper river. But if colder water temperatures hurt some aquatic species, they doubtless helped others. In the course of our day astream we witnessed a succession of hatches that included several types of mayflies (the Green Drake, *Ephemerella glacialis,* and a small red quill that eluded my taxonomic skills) as well as swarms of caddis and the occasional little green or yellow stone fly.

When it came to stream entomology, Fothergill's knowledge was strictly practical—he knew as much as he needed to help him catch fish. Like all accomplished anglers, he had mastered the skills of effective presentation, and the flies he preferred were impressionistic—the Gold-Ribbed Hare's Ear, Muskrat, Renegade, and so on—rather than patterns meant to mimic particular insects.

In his forty-plus years of angling, Fothergill had retained his child's enthusiasm for catching fish, whether they were fourteen-inch rainbows on the Frying Pan or hundred-pound tarpon in Costa Rica. Besides tarpon and bonefish in Central America, he told me, he had pursued Atlantic salmon in Iceland and Scotland as well as trout in England, Pakistan, New Zealand, and throughout the Rocky Mountain West. But his loyalty to his home waters remained unswerving. "I believe that the Frying Pan and Roaring Fork are equal or superior to many Montana rivers from the point of view of their insect life and numbers of fish," he said. And unlike rivers such as the Yellowstone or the Bighorn, which may be a hundred yards or more across and unfishable except by floating, his rivers were relatively intimate and accessible to the wading angler. As he put it, "They are *friendly* streams."

Under Fothergill's tutelage I was beginning to learn just how friendly. The next afternoon, armed with such insight as I'd managed to glean from our day's fishing together, I tried the Frying Pan on my own. It was another brilliant Colorado day with the same succession of hatches we had seen before. Fishing some of the productive places Fothergill had shown me, I caught and released a baker's dozen in perhaps five hours on the water—a respectable if not spectacular showing, and one that only suggested the river's potential for a knowledgeable angler. A final brace of rainbows came at dusk, in a narrow run guarded by a stand of spruce. Slipping the hook from the last fish and watching it dart back into deeper water, I marveled again at its deep-bellied strength and the vigor of its run and pirouettes.

## SEVEN

# Al Troth of the Beaverhead

In January 1988 I fished for two days on the slopes of Mount Kenya, where limpid creeks course through a fantastic moorland of heather and tussock grass and palmlike giant lobelia. One doesn't think of finding trout on the equator, yet the creeks of Mount Kenya are chockablock with small brown trout, the feral descendants of fish stocked decades ago by British colonials. Finning in the heads of pools under a cloudless sky, with a clear view of predators in the treeless landscape, these wild and wary fish aren't the easiest to catch. Yet with persistence, and with help from one of the world's great flies, I managed to hook and release a score of them.

Seven months later, in Dillon, Montana, I met the father of the fly that had fooled my African trout. When I told Al Troth about my success with his Elkhair Caddis, his grizzled face lit up.

I had driven over to Troth's place (the "Home of the Elkhair Caddis," as it says in large letters on the outside of his workshop) from the campground where I was staying during my first trip to the Beaverhead, when I fished it with Tim Tollett and the spirit of Silas Goodrich. A squarely built man with a peppery beard, a long nose, and a complexion made ruddy by long days of guiding on the river, Troth greeted me brusquely. He hadn't really wanted to see me when I'd called asking for an interview, for it was his first day off from guiding in weeks and he had lots to do. He'd been on the phone most of the morning with clients, and that hadn't improved his mood, either.

"The most frustrating thing about guiding," he told me as he sorted through tackle and other gear in his garage, "is taking out people with little ability, who think, because they're paying you, that they should have instant success. In too many cases they can't cast and sometimes I have to tie their flies and leaders on—they can't even do basic stuff. I've got this habit of punching my watch whenever people tie on tippets and flies. I tell 'em, learn to tie quickly so you don't waste time on the river, especially when you have thirty minutes of daylight left and the trout are going crazy. This guy yesterday—you know how long it took him? Fourteen minutes! I took the same fly and tied it on myself in forty-one seconds!" Shaking his head, he began counting on his fingers. "Yesterday we saw one, two, three . . . fourteen fish twenty inches or better feeding. We caught two of 'em."

After a particularly frustrating day, Troth has been known to tell a client never to call him again. But as I would learn, whatever he expected of his clients was no less than what he demanded of himself. His approach to fly-fishing recalled Vince Lombardi's to football and George Patton's to war. His commitment was total, and he believed that if you tend to the details, the rest will take care of itself.

As Chuck Walton, a friend and longtime angling companion of Troth's, told me, "He's a perfectionist. He's German, and like most Germans, he sets a very high standard of performance. As a guide, he's so determined to have you catch fish. If you're receptive to Al's way of teaching, you can really learn. He'll push you, and sometimes people don't like that. I know two fishermen he guided recently. One responded beautifully to Al and caught a lot of fish. The other didn't respond at all and actually left the boat for an hour."

It was two years before I could return to the Beaverhead and actually fish it with Troth. The afternoon before our scheduled float, he took me to Clark Canyon Reservoir for some float-tubing. As we drove south on the Interstate in his pickup truck, he filled me in on his background. Troth's compulsion to do things right came from his father, a machinist in Monessen, a steel town near Pittsburgh. The son spent much of his childhood in his dad's shop. Troth Sr. taught his only child to use a lathe and a milling machine and to check the results with a micrometer. Al applied the same care and precision when he began tying trout flies, using a fly-tying kit given to his father by a hard up customer in lieu of cash. He taught himself to tie by unraveling store-bought flies. "I was a member of the junior rifle club. Our instructor was a fly fisherman, and he gave me some English flies he'd purchased at Abercrombie's or a Chicago store," he recalled. "They were good examples to match, so my fly tying was probably a notch above from the start."

The same instructor introduced him to fly-fishing. Troth fished and hunted in the mountains of western Pennsylvania through high school, worked as a metallurgist in a steel mill, spent four years in the navy, picked up a B.A. in education from a teacher's college near home, then moved to Williamsport in central Pennsylvania, where he taught industrial arts to high school kids for fifteen years while honing his angling skills on the region's demanding waters.

It was in central Pennsylvania that Troth developed the Elkhair Caddis to imitate a green caddis hatch he found on Big Pine Creek, Penns Creek, and the Loyalsock. The pattern and his technique for tying it were influenced by the writings of G. E. M. Skues, a great turn-of-the century British angler and the first modern theorist on nymph fishing. "Skues had a dry fly pattern he called the Little Red Sedge, and I liked the way he tied it," he recalled. Skues began by tying in gold wire at the rear of the hook; then he dubbed the body, tied in the hackle near the front of the hook, wound the hackle back over the body, wound the wire forward through the hackle, and winged the fly with wood duck. Troth followed Skues's method, but in place of the wood duck he substituted the lighter colored, stiffer hair of a bull elk, flared 180 degrees so that it acted as an outrigger. (He eventually came to prefer the hair of a cow elk, which he bleached for greater visibility.) Although designed to imitate a caddis fly, the Elkhair—like other time-tested flies such as the Muddler Minnow, the Adams, and the Hare's Ear and Pheasant Tail nymphs—has become a great generic pattern. "It'll imitate stone flies, little hoppers, any number of things," said Troth, who tied his first Elkhair in 1957. "The trout ate it then, they eat it now, and they'll eat it twenty years from now."

By 1961, Troth was tying the Elkhair and other patterns commercially and selling them through Bud Lilly's Tackle Shop in West Yellowstone, Montana. In the summers, he lived in West Yellowstone and guided for Lilly on the Madison and in Yellowstone Park. In 1973, he quit teaching and moved to Montana for good with his wife, Martha, and son, Eric. "My only mistake was in not moving out here sooner," he said. "Martha was the initiator. She told me, 'I don't like that long ride out every summer.' I asked, 'What'll I do to make a living?' She said, 'You'll think of something.'"

They chose Dillon, an agricultural, mining, and timber town of 5,000 people, for its proximity to the Beaverhead and Big Hole Rivers. While Martha worked as a substitute teacher,

Al tied flies and guided. To supplement their earnings he branched into outdoor photography and began building and selling a portable deer stand for bow hunters and a hackle gauge for flytiers, which he sold through Dan Bailey's.

Arriving at Clark Canyon Dam, we left the Interstate and took a secondary road along the western edge of the reservoir. At the Horse Prairie access we turned off the road and drove down a shelving beach toward shore. The lake level was way down, a result of the drought that had gripped southwestern Montana for the previous three years. Troth worried it would mean another fall of drastically reduced water releases for the Beaverhead.

The day was cold and blustery, and the fitful sun played hide-and-seek behind rain clouds rolling across the sere hills. When the sun came out, its reflection backlighted the float-tubers adrift on the lake. In silhouette, and with no nearby objects to lend scale, they looked like a flotilla of tugboats. We joined some fishermen down by the water. Huddled in their rain gear and sipping coffee from a thermos, they chatted amiably. Their vans bore license plates from South Carolina, Georgia, and Missouri. They included several retired couples who had driven over from Hebgen Lake, on the Madison. The group came out here every summer, we learned, and tubing for trout was the only fishing they did. Their tubes were state-of-the-art and driven by battery-powered motors. It was my first inkling that such an angling subculture existed. I pondered the aptness of the name tubers—the piscatorial equivalent of couch potatoes.

This was my first experience with tubing, and I wasn't confident that much would come of it. The fishing had been slow, they said, which I took to mean that no one had caught anything. As we donned our waders, I asked Troth about tactics. "You can paddle a little faster or a little slower, and you can work the line a little, but basically you're just trolling," he said. Slipping on my fins, I concluded that I had just been told at least 50 percent of all I would ever need to know about tubing.

I managed to get into the tube and launch from the shore without capsizing. Out on the water, I got off a splashy cast. I was fishing a Prince Nymph. Although Troth told me to use a 5X tippet, I cheated and opted for stouter 3X. It took only a few minutes to become accustomed to being suspended chest deep in the surprisingly warm water. Drifting downwind, lulled by the sound of waves slapping against the tube, I leaned back and watched the scudding clouds and the occasional pelican beating overhead. There could be worse ways of not catching fish.

*Wham!*

My rod surged to the pull of a strong fish. Like an anvil with fins, it plunged and bulldogged and ran in a circle around the tube. I yelled to Troth, who paddled over and slipped me his net so I could land the fish while he took photos.

"Get closer to me!" he said. "You're paddling the wrong way!" He was right—I couldn't figure out how to face him for the benefit of the camera while at the same time propelling myself in his direction.

"Just stay where you are and I'll come to you!"

The fish I finally hefted in the net was a thick hen rainbow of eighteen inches. Sometime later, I was dozing off again when another fish took. It went deep into my backing and, from what seemed an unimaginable distance, I watched it leap once and break off. The third and last fish of the afternoon was a cock rainbow of three pounds, which Troth netted for me. In the process I hooked my fly in his brand-new neoprene waders.

We drove up the Interstate again the next day, this time hauling Troth's neoprene raft to float the river. In prime condition, the eleven-mile stretch of the river below Clark Canyon

Dam supports upwards of nineteen hundred large trout per mile. Reduced water flows caused by the prolonged drought had stressed the fish and killed some of the bigger trout, said Troth, "but the Beaverhead is such a great fishery that even when it's bad, it's good."

Al called a good day on the Beaverhead landing three fish of four pounds or better. On one exceptional day, he said, a client hooked twelve fish over four pounds, all on the Elkhair Caddis, and landed seven. Like other Beaverhead guides, when talking about the size of fish he tended to go by weight rather than length, and he dismissed the "snaky" trout of lesser rivers. As I had seen with Tim Tollett two years before, the upper Beaverhead's nutrient-rich waters and constant temperature result in high growth rates and trout with the oblateness of rugby balls. A typical twenty-inch brown or rainbow averages better than three pounds, and the occasional hawg tips the scales at four.

We launched the raft at the first highway bridge below the dam. Before starting our float, Troth suggested we try a few casts in a feeding lie behind one of the bridge pilings. It was 10:30 A.M., and some pale morning duns were beginning to show, although there was no sign of fish feeding on the surface. We started with a size-sixteen Pheasant Tail Nymph fished upstream, with a foam strike indicator pinched to the leader. Troth positioned himself opposite the feeding lane to spot the fish and direct my casting: "Your indicator landed on his dorsal . . . go up two feet and one foot to the left. Good cast. You got him!" The first fish ran downstream with me splashing in pursuit, but the hook pulled out. The second fish, an eighteen-inch rainbow, I managed to maneuver into the shallows, where Troth scooped it up in his two-handed net. We admired it briefly before releasing it.

With the pressure off—at least now I wouldn't be skunked—I felt my confidence rising. It didn't hurt, of course, being coached by the Dean of the Beaverhead, and the trout were cooperating too. As we moved down river, they seemed to be feeding in every lie we stopped to fish. Our routine was to park the boat and work the water on foot. We found a pod of large fish in a side channel. The first trout rattled me when it exploded from the water, took off across stream, and jumped again near the far bank. With my line stretched the width of the river, I watched a McKenzie boat drifting down toward it. The trout refrained from taking advantage of my predicament and obligingly ran back across the river. But just as I began to think we might land it, the trout lunged and broke off.

Al noted a major flaw in the way I had played the fish. When a trout runs, my instinct is to lower the rod. "Hold your rod tip high!" he said. "If you doubt what I'm saying, try an experiment at home sometime: tie a leader to a fence post and see how much pressure it takes to break it while holding the rod back at two o'clock. Then hold the rod down at ten o'clock and see what it takes." Holding the rod back, as I would learn, maximizes the tip's cushioning effect, while holding it low transfers the strain to the stiffer butt. His other advice on playing strong, wild fish: "Get them in the quiet water next to the shore. If they get in the middle of the river and run, they've got you by the short hairs."

Applying these lessons, I took several more fish. Then I hooked into a bruiser brown that veered into the fast water and cleared the surface in a leap. My heart leapt with it. I reeled in the slack and slid one hand up the rod, leveraging the trout into the side water. Troth waded in behind the fish, but his net had wrapped around its frame, and he was having trouble untangling it. For some reason he thought this was funny and, while I cursed under my breath, he chuckled. Meanwhile, the trout shot back into the main current and ripped downstream, melting line off the reel. My backing was about gone when I suggested that perhaps we ought to get in the boat and follow. Troth pondered this. "Well, I don't know. There must be ten fish working here—I hate to leave such a good spot." He looked at the lengthening hypotenuse of my line and took pity. "OK, let's go." Leaning on the oars, he began telling a story about another client in a similar situation, but before he finished, the fish plunged into a chute and broke off.

Al Troth's enjoyment in being on the river belied the impression he gave when he talked about guiding, a service business whose attractions—being your own boss and spending every day on a trout stream—are offset by a marginal income and brutal hours.

"It's a piss-poor way to make a living," he told me. "You might charge $200 a day, but if you work out of a fly shop the owner takes his cut, and $30 of every $100 you make goes to the state for workers' compensation. Then there's the cost of your boat, trailer registration, and insurance. After all that, you're lucky to be making $100 a day. I could do better cutting lawns." As for the hours, he said, "You're up at 5:30 getting ready, and a lot of times you're not off the river till ten o'clock at night. You get five hours' sleep and you're up the next morning to do it all over again. I've been on the water twenty-one out of the last twenty-three days. I usually guide at least a hundred days a year, and I've been doing it since 1972. Before you know it, you're old and gray and feel like you're following a mule."

Al was sixty-one years old, an age when most people are thinking of retirement. But the concept seemed alien to Troth, who, despite grousing about it, clearly thrived on his regimen.

As often as not, days off found him returning to the river, either to fish or take photographs, often teaming with his son, Eric, to shoot pictures for fishing and hunting magazines.

The estimated thousand-plus hours he spent annually on the Beaverhead dovetailed with his other main vocation. "To be a good flytier," said Troth, "you have to be on the river and see what's going on."

He had 150 regular customers for his flies (they included media maven and fly-fishing convert Ted Turner) and a waiting list estimated at 450: "Somebody has to die before somebody else gets a spot in there," he said. Later, I spent some time with him in his tying room, and it was obvious that he took the same methodical approach to fly tying that he did with everything else. His bench was a monument to Teutonic order, with hackles sorted by type and size and stored in labeled glassine envelopes arrayed on a board in front of him. For tying the Elkhair Caddis and Pheasant Tail Nymph, he used custom-made gold wire tempered to his specifications. He knew to the second how long each pattern took, and he was compulsive about consistency. "I always look for the easy technique," he said. "Once I've sorted materials, most flies take me between two and a half and four and a half minutes to tie. I've got the specs of all my patterns filed on index cards. If you placed an order with me ten years ago for a fly that had nine turns of lead wire with a diameter of fifteen-thousandths of an inch, that's exactly what it'll have if you order it today."

During our float, the fly that worked best was a white caddis pupa dressed in size sixteen, but on a size-fourteen hook. He had yet to name the pattern, and it did not appear in the modest catalog he published. "I may use a fly for a couple of years and make sure it's successful before it gets a name and goes in the catalog," he said.

I was fishing Al's Pupa (we'll call it that) late in the afternoon over a fish feeding a foot below the surface in a narrow run. Troth had pointed it out to me from the embankment overlooking the spot. While I slid down to take position behind the fish, he stayed on the embankment to guide my casting. I had a good fix on the fish, and on the second or third cast the current swallowed my strike indicator. An instant after I set the hook, the biggest, fattest, darkest trout of the day burst from the surface and fell back, hitting the water like a steam iron.

"You got him!" yelled Troth.

The fish went broadside to the current and sounded. Forgetting everything he had taught me, I dipped the rod and almost instantly felt the tippet snap. From over my shoulder I could hear the words before they were out of his mouth.

"Oh—you—dropped—your—*rod!*"

I felt like a high school football player blasted by his coach for fumbling on the goal line.

"I couldn't help it," I said. As an excuse it was even lamer than it sounded.

But the waning afternoon yielded several more fish, and by dusk, when Troth cranked the winch on his trailer, hauling the raft from the pewter current, I'd landed and released eight of fourteen trout, all but two between eighteen and twenty-one inches. I was happy but bone tired, and my head throbbed. Yet Troth seemed as fresh as the morning, and he was still going strong—talking about fishing, photography, bow hunting, and other outdoor stuff—when we arrived back at his place. When I shook hands and thanked him for the best day I'd ever had on a trout stream, he paid me the ultimate compliment: "You're a pleasure to fish with," he said.

I fairly floated back to my campsite. The next day, after sleeping late, I was packed and on my way. Departing Dillon, I glanced at my watch. It was ten o'clock. Al Troth, I knew, was back on the river.

## EIGHT

*Dennis Black: Lord of the Flies*

Dennis Black had an idea. For years, retail fly shops had complained to him about running out of popular patterns midway through the fishing season and being unable to restock their bins until the following winter, long after the immediate need had passed.

Black understood the problem well enough, for as a professional flytier he was part of it. Like most people in this cottage industry, he tied flies all winter to fill the preseason orders from retail shops. In the spring he went fishing. Later in the season, when the shops screamed for more flies, he would be loath to leave the stream to return to his fly-tying bench. It was important to keep your priorities straight, after all, and tying flies was only a means to an end.

The solution to this perennial fix emerged after Black quit tying flies himself and founded Umpqua Feather Merchants.

That was in 1974. By 1987, when I interviewed him for an Angler of the Year profile for *Rod & Reel* magazine, his company had become the nation's largest importer of quality flies. Although he zealously guarded his annual production figures, the number of flies turned out by his overseas factories was well into the millions. While most of Umpqua's thousand or so customers were small mom-and-pop shops—the backbone of the industry—the firm also supplied L. L. Bean, Gander Mountain, Kaufmann's, Orvis, and other large houses. The trade magazine *Fly-Tackle Dealer* estimated that half the flies sold in the United States originated from Umpqua Feather Merchants.

The soft-spoken Black, who was forty-seven when I met him at the firm's headquarters in Glide, Oregon, had come a long way from his days as a freelance flytier. There was a period in the early 1970s when he and his kid brother, Bill, lived in a cabin in the Umpqua National Forest. Dennis tied flies and Bill made jewelry. Both wore ponytails, and in the spring they would load Dennis's winter output of flies into his 1964 Volkswagen van and head to Wyoming and Montana, selling the flies and fishing.

Dennis Black's salt-and-pepper hair was cut short now, and he wore a neatly trimmed mustache. While he no longer looked like a hippie, no one would have mistaken him for a Fortune 500 executive either, despite his heading a business that was chugging along with an annual growth rate of 25 to 40 percent. Dressed in running shoes and hiking shorts, he was a big, full-framed man whose broad fists and broken nose suggested he could hold his own in a bar fight. The rest of Umpqua's thirty-two employees were dressed with equal casualness, and I noticed rigged fly rods in every corner; nearly everyone who worked there also fished, and the North Umpqua River was less than a minute's drive away—close enough to catch a steelhead on your lunch hour.

When I arrived in Glide, a blink-and-miss-it logging town at the west entrance to the Umpqua National Forest, I drove around for at least an hour trying to find Black's operation. Although perched on a rise and plainly visible from the road, Umpqua Feather Merchants had no sign, and when I asked for directions few people in Glide seemed even to have heard of it. I finally located the single-story metal building that just two years before had housed an assembly plant for satellite dish antennas. Before that, I learned, it had been a worm farm.

The low profile was deliberate, Black told me—he didn't want fishermen thinking the place was a retail outlet for Umpqua flies. This hardly seemed a problem, for at the time, Umpqua was hardly a household name. There were thousands of anglers out there armed to the gills with Umpqua flies who didn't even know the line existed. Most retailers didn't specify the origins of the flies they sold, and anyway, they didn't want customers knowing their flies came from overseas—a hangover from an era when "foreign made" meant cheap, gaudy flies that unraveled on the second cast.

This was a notion that Black had turned on its head. The Umpqua line, he stated flatly, now "sets the standard for quality in American flies." There were several reasons for this, he asserted. Although Umpqua's seven hundred patterns were being tied in overseas factories by women who may not have grasped even the concept of fly-fishing, the company maintained exceptional quality through training, supervision, and the selection of materials. The flies were all tied on chemically sharpened Tiemco hooks, and dry flies used top-of-the-line Metz and Hoffman hackles. Virtually all materials originated in the United States. On a tour, my jaw dropped at the sight of entire crate loads of elk and deer hides awaiting shipment overseas.

Black had built up his overseas operation to include more than three hundred tiers working in four different factories— three in the Far East (Sri Lanka, India, and Mauritius) and one in South America (Colombia). A fifth factory, in Thailand, would soon begin operations. Umpqua was a part owner in several of the factories and had deals with the others to take all their production in exchange for quality control.

When Umpqua began importing top-grade flies in staggering numbers, some American flytiers accused Black of exploiting cheap foreign labor—a charge he vigorously denied. "Our girls do as well or better than workers in comparable industries in the countries where we do business, and they all have benefits—vacations, bonuses, sick pay, and maternity leave. Some of these girls are supporting their entire families, and it's not making slaves of them—it gives them freedom. I think it's beneficial to encourage free enterprise in Third World countries." He was equally emphatic when responding to complaints that he has taken business away from American tiers: "We've encouraged the growth of fly-fishing by making quality flies available in numbers that satisfy the market. And that benefits everybody."

Dennis Black's Southern California origins held little hint of his future role as an angling entrepreneur. He grew up in Long Beach, the oldest of five brothers. Married and a father by the time he graduated from high school, he didn't even consider college. Instead, he found a job in Fresno managing a warehouse for Tupperware. One day a friend came through on his way home from Montana with a freezer chest full of trout he'd caught there. It got Black thinking about fishing, something he'd never done but thought he might like to try. His father-in-law lent him a fly rod. Black bought some flies— ironically, he recalled, they were "three-for-a-quarter" cheapos from Taiwan—and went up into the Sierra Nevada and caught some fish. He was hooked.

Black credited several people with nurturing his interest in fly-fishing and fly tying, a hobby that soon turned into a semiprofession. Wayne "Buzz" Buszek, a professional tier in Visalia, taught him the fine points of his craft. "I learned to tie flies out of books, then met Buzz—what a difference watching him made." Black kept at his bench for up to four hours at a stretch, turning out hundreds of flies—all of which he gave away. "I thought selling them would take away the enjoyment." One beneficiary of his largess was Ed Strickland, a founder of the Federation of Fly Fishers, who finally convinced Black to accept payment. Soon he was selling to other individuals, then to retail shops. Meanwhile, he had begun exploring the fishing in the Cascades of northern California and Oregon, and on a trip to the Trinity River he caught his first steelhead.

With a wife and five kids to support, Black was sensible enough not to quit his daytime job at Tupperware. But on the side, between fishing trips, he continued to expand his fly tying business. In his first venture, he founded Black's Custom Flies and soon had a stable of other part-timers tying for him. These included brother Bill, still a teenager living at home, and future fly shop owners Randall Kaufmann and Jack Dennis, whom Black met in the back room of a sporting goods store in Jackson, Wyoming. "Randall, Jack, and I used to have races to see who could tie the most flies in the shortest time," he remembered. "It got so we could do simple patterns like a Zug Bug or a Tellico in fifty seconds."

By 1968 he was making more money tying flies than at his regular job. Realizing that his fortune probably lay in fur and feathers rather than in plastic, he gave Tupperware notice and packed his family off to Oregon, settling near Roseburg, on the North Umpqua River. "My routine was to get up at six, tie for four hours, take a break and catch a couple of steelhead, then go back to tying."

Over the next several years the business expanded. Branching into wholesale materials, he began importing hackle necks from India and convinced a friend, Henry Hoffman, to raise genetically bred grizzly necks commercially. Black became the exclusive distributor of Hoffman necks, which quickly established themselves as a benchmark for quality hackle. Through his Indian connections, meanwhile, he imported his first foreign-made flies. Fate—in the form of a leaky oil burner that sent his business up in flames—convinced him to phase out of commercial fly tying and focus on importing materials. That was in December 1973. Within a few months, he recalled, "I had an opportunity to buy a bunch of chicken necks in India. I began going there and handpicking them, so the quality was always good. My dad and a brother lent me some money, which allowed me to establish Umpqua Feather Merchants." Meanwhile, he began to expand his incipient business of importing quality flies made to his specifications with American materials—in particular the superb Hoffman hackles. "My arrangement with Hoffman gave me exclusive rights to his necks, and there was no one else in the country at the time producing hackle nearly as good. I could walk into shops and show them flies that nobody could match, because I was the only one with access to Hoffman necks."

From the first, Dennis added, "the whole point of the importing business was to offer quality flies." The quantity of flies went up as Hoffman expanded its operation and more top-grade necks became available.

As Umpqua Feather Merchants continued to grow, Black managed to avoid the "founder's disease" that afflicts entrepreneurs who excel at starting companies but fail at running them. When we spoke in 1987, he declined to predict the true size of his market niche. "When we were doing a tenth of the business we are now I wondered if we were reaching the saturation point," he said. "Every year I ask, 'How much bigger can we get?' I just don't know."

Black spent most of the year overseas, working from the house he owned in Sri Lanka. "I'm lucky to be two months at home," he said. "But the key to doing business in the Far East is established relations. The more time you spend there, the easier it goes." I was able to see him now because it was July and the summer steelhead season, which he never misses, had started on the North Umpqua. After nearly twenty years on the river, he knew its fishery—a mix of wild and hatchery stocks—as well as anyone. Then as now, the North Umpqua boasted one of the best summer steelhead runs in the continental United States (some 20,000 had ascended the river the previous summer, and this year's run appeared to be comparable), and Dennis agreed to introduce me to the water. It would be my first experience fishing for the great sea-run rainbows of the Pacific.

Spawned near Crater Lake in the Cascades, the North Umpqua courses seventy miles to its junction with the main river, below Roseburg. Above Glide it is a canyon river of arresting beauty, plunging past basalt cliffs and through towering stands of Douglas fir, its green pools beckoning. The Diamond Lake Highway, a two-lane logging road that hugs the canyon walls as it follows the river's twists and turns, offers commanding vistas. Fishermen wading the edges of the North Umpqua's sweeping bends look dwarfed and superfluous—anglers in a Bierstadt landscape. Few of the world's rivers can match the North Umpqua in its combination of big fish and spectacular scenery. Zane Grey, who fished it near the end of his life (he was felled by a stroke on it in 1937), rated its fishing "superior to any river in the United States, and comparable only to the great rivers of Newfoundland or the far-famed Tongariro of New Zealand."

When we got to the river, I hurriedly pulled on my waders while Black glassed the water for steelhead. He asked about my experience playing large fish: "You've fished for Atlantic salmon, I assume?" I said no. "What's the biggest trout you've ever caught, then?" I told him seventeen inches (this was before my first trip to the Beaverhead). A look of concern crossed his face—North Umpqua steelhead generally run twenty-four to thirty-six inches and weigh six to twelve pounds, with thirty inches and eight pounds being average. (Black's biggest, caught in August 1985 on a size-four purple Zonker, was thirty-seven inches and sixteen pounds.) I assured him that I had caught plenty of medium-sized trout on small flies and 7X tippets. "It's just a matter of scaling up."

The water was a tailout, the lower end of a pool at the top of a long rapid. Black explained that steelhead usually move quickly through a rapid, then rest in the quieter holding lies above it. Once he pointed them out, I could see the shadowy forms of five steelhead hanging in the current. I fished through the run without success. When I finished, Black took my place. With a long, effortless cast, he placed his floating line above the pod and mended upstream to sink the weighted Woolly Bugger. With the rod tip he followed the line through its drift, and at the end gave it a few twitches.

On his third cast he was fast to a steelhead. With rod bent and line peeling out, he turned to me. "Do you want to play him?"

I hesitated only a second. "Sure!"

I grabbed the rod. The fish had stopped running, and I began stripping in line.

"No, no—play him from the reel!"

Immediately the line went slack.

"He's off," I said.

"Don't worry," Dennis consoled. "Happens all the time."

So it went. On my own, I fished hard over the next two days but came up blank. I caught a few juvenile fish in the eight-to-ten-inch category and broke off a fly in one adult steelhead at the instant of setting the hook. I took solace in what I had read and heard about the difficulty of this fishing. Ray Bergman, who fished the North Umpqua in the 1940s, hooked five fish on his first three days on the river and lost them all. (Not very convincingly, Bergman declared that the fish that got away were always the ones "that thrill me the most. So I say it is good to lose fish.") Dick Bauer, president of the Steamboaters, a group of North Umpqua conservationists, told me he could go five or six days without a hookup, then get six or seven fish on his line without landing a single one. Even Black admitted he was still learning, although by Umpqua standards his success was extraordinary—he counted on striking a fish in at least every other pool, and managed to land more than half of those hooked. "The new, harder leader materials are much more abrasion resistant and have made a big difference in landing fish," he said. "Still, it's tough fishing, but after twenty years it's not near as tough as it was in the first few years. After you've done it a while you learn the places where bigger fish hold. You can get addicted to 'buck hunting'—fishing just for the larger fish."

By my third and last day on the river I would have settled for even a small steelhead. I had learned to read the water better and felt more confident in my wading and casting. By midafternoon, after seven hours of fishing, I was tiring and fighting to keep my concentration. I was working a deep cut in a bedrock reef, methodically quartering my line upstream and mending to get the fly down, as Black had showed me. On the second cast the line stopped short. I lifted the rod and felt the hook dig in.

In a steady, majestic motion the steelhead pulled away. The line ran through the rod guides, and faster than I could do anything about it the loops of line I'd been holding closed tight around my fingers. My hand snubbed against the stripping guide. The rod dipped, the line stopped, the leader snapped.

After shouting and screaming for a while, I calmed down. I was still a steelhead virgin and resigned to remaining so for the foreseeable future. I climbed out of the river and trudged back to the car, which was parked upstream of the Steamboat Inn (a favorite watering hole for steelheaders, named after a nearby spawning tributary). A historical marker read:

## STEAMBOAT

Renowned for its fly-fishing for summer steelhead.
A favorite fishing spot of famed author Zane Grey
named for the mining term "steamboated,"
an area that didn't pan out.

I thought of Dennis Black and the other anglers fortunate
enough to fish the North Umpqua regularly. I envied them and
felt sure I would return.

## NINE

*Penn State's*
*Other Joe*

It was a bright spring afternoon on Fisherman's Paradise, a stretch of Spring Creek near State College, Pennsylvania, and Professor Joe Humphreys was hard at work.

Wearing his trademark PSU ball cap, Humphreys moved along the stream, fly rod in hand, scanning the water for fish. "There's one right next to the rock down there, and another," he said, pointing out a pair of finning trout to the dozen students following along behind him. "Remember what we learned in class. The fish are tight to the bank here because there's a good velocity change, and this is where the food is—there're more sow and cress bugs here than out in the current."

Farther downstream, the students paused as Humphreys removed a rock from the stream and turned it over, examining the insects on its bottom. After the briefest of entomology lessons—he pointed out some sulphur nymphs and a couple of caddis worms wrapped in detritus—he returned the rock to the water and announced: "It's time now for some fun."

"Fun" for Humphreys is fly-fishing on the demanding spring creeks and limestone streams of central Pennsylvania, and for the next hour he demonstrated a few of the basic skills he had learned in a half century of angling for some of the world's most discriminating trout. His audience comprised the students in his fly-fishing course at Penn State University. This first day of April 1986 was their first day on a stream after two months in the classroom learning the fundamentals of casting, fly tying, stream ecology, and trout behavior. While most of them had some prior angling experience, all but a few were new to fishing with a fly.

These weren't the easiest conditions for catching fish. The water was relatively low and clear for so early in the year, and Humphreys had the added burden of delivering a non-stop lecture. He began by tying on a sculpin pattern and snubbing a split shot against its nose. The weight and its location, he explained, "gives the fly some action—it'll dive and dart like a little jig." From the bank, he worked the fly in a series of short casts through a half dozen fish holding in a few inches of water in a weedy side channel, varying the speed of the retrieve and lengthening his casts until all the water was covered. The trout turned and inspected the pattern but refused to take it. "You'll have some days when they'll just touch and tease with it and others when they'll really go for it," he said.

With his students in tow he moved over to the main channel, this time for some upstream nymphing and a demonstration of the tuck cast, a method developed by Humphreys's friend and mentor, George Harvey, for dropping a weighted nymph to the water before the line. Shoulders hunched, he kept his rod hand close to his face and leaned into the cast, then followed the drifting line with the concentration of a heron. In short order he was into a fish—a small rainbow that he quickly landed and released. A few casts later he hooked a slightly larger brown, followed by a fifteen-inch rainbow in spawning colors.

In a few more minutes it was time for the students to board the bus for the ride back to campus, but before they went, Humphreys wanted a try at several of the trout he had spotted earlier. He walked upstream and knelt close to the water while the class watched intently from the high bank. After several casts, the nearer of two steadily rising fish came to the fly, but Humphreys missed the strike. "I've got him moving!" he said as he changed to a small nymph. He cast several more times, got his backcast caught on a bush, broke off and changed flies again, and resumed casting. "I've got ten minutes to catch a fish!"

When, a few casts later, the fish rose to the small fly and was hooked, several students applauded.

"Alright!"

"Thataway, Humph!"

Humphreys brought in the struggling fish, a gleaming brown of about fifteen inches. He beamed at it for a moment before slipping the hook and releasing it.

"We've got to get out of here!" he exclaimed, but the other trout was still rising and he couldn't resist a few hurried, fruitless casts before at last reeling in and heading toward the bus.

Although focused on technique, Humphreys's demonstration along the elm-lined banks of Fisherman's Paradise exemplified other, more fundamental qualities of the successful angler: concentration, persistence, and perhaps above all a *will* to catch fish.

Like love and marriage, fly-fishing has several stages. For most anglers, an early romance with their sport eventually gives way to a deeper, more intimate familiarity. Not so for Joe Humphreys. His affair with trout had gone on for five decades by the time I met him, but in all that time none of the passion had faded. At age fifty-seven he still had trout lust. Joe's obsession recalled the words of his friend, the late Vince Marinaro, who in *A Modern Dry-Fly Code* likened his own feelings toward trout fishing to those of a hound "joyously baying in full, hot pursuit of its quarry."

Humphreys's own pursuit of trout began in these same Pennsylvania hills at age five, not long after his family moved to State College from nearby Curvinsville. "My father went to work as a clerk in the burser's office at Penn State after losing his bank job in the crash of '29," he remembered. "He wanted to be able to send his kids to college and figured that was one way to do it. My brother, who was seven years older, introduced me to fishing. I caught my first trout at age six—age five was a bad year, I guess—and my first on a fly at age eight or nine.

"The fishing around here was wonderful," he added. "Close to home we had Thompson's Spring Creek and Slab Cabin Run, which entered Spring Creek just below town. After school we'd jump on our bicycles and pedal down there, our fly rods across the handlebars, and fish from three-thirty until dark. There were also little brook trout streams in the mountains, and on Saturdays we'd pack lunches and ride up there to fish. We had the best of both worlds—limestone creeks in the valley and freestoners in the mountains."

Limestone streams, while rare in North America relative to the more common freestone streams, are abundant in central Pennsylvania. As trout habitat they have several advantages, all related to the qualities of limestone formations: steady flow, cool temperatures, and a rich supply of insects for the trout to feed on. The abundance of feed and the slow, clear water typical of limestone streams make for finicky, spooky trout that can be the ultimate test of an angler's skill.

In addition to being blessed by access to some of the East's best trout water, young Joe could look to some of its best fly fishermen as role models. Among these local anglers schooled in the art of limestone fishing was George Harvey, a physical education instructor at Penn State who introduced a course in angling—the country's first such college course—at about the same time Humphreys's family moved to State College. Harvey, he recalled, encouraged him and other youngsters in their fishing and "always had a kind word of advice."

After high school and service in the navy, Humphreys entered Penn State, where he not only took George Harvey's course but helped him teach it. A physical education major and a nationally ranked college wrestler and boxer, Humphreys went on to a coaching career at several Pennsylvania high schools before returning to his alma mater in 1970 as a coach and physical education instructor. He shared teaching the angling course with Harvey until the latter's retirement in 1973. By 1986, Humphreys was teaching five sections of the course (with about twenty-five students per section) as well as a course devoted exclusively to casting. By then Joe Paterno, the school's great football coach, had reached legendary status, but Penn State's other Joe was a sporting legend in his own right.

The fly-fishing course—P.E. 109, Principles and Techniques of Angling—met once a week for fifteen weeks. Each session lasted two hours and fifty minutes and was divided between a lecture (usually augmented by a film or videotape) and a fly tying "laboratory." In the lectures, Humphreys discoursed on such topics as water temperature and its effect on trout, fly hatches, strategy, casting, and leaders and knots. The themes of sportsmanship and conservation ran through all the materials. There were field trips, like the one to Fisherman's Paradise, but no homework and usually only one quiz during the semester. The final exam had a written part and two fly tying problems.

Penn State required each of its 36,000 undergraduates to earn three physical education credits to graduate, and for many of Humphreys's students the course was a pleasant and not especially demanding way of fulfilling part of the P.E. requirement. If Principles and Techniques of Angling lacked the academic rigor of, say, organic chemistry or advanced calculus, that was fine with Humphreys. "I tell them we're here to have fun," he said. "In these stressful times, a course like this has the greatest carryover value in the world. We're teaching these kids a way to appreciate the outdoors and introducing them to something they can enjoy for the rest of their lives."

A typical class began with a lecture and slide presentation. On the morning preceding the outing at Fisherman's Paradise, the topic was strategy by degrees. Humphreys moved briskly through the materials, from optimal feeding temperatures for trout to the hydrology of limestone and freestone creeks to techniques for locating spring seeps where trout congregate during the dog days of summer. Slides flashed on the screen—charts and diagrams, photos of feeding trout, and pretty views of streams accompanied by a tape-recorded pastorale. The mixed-media show continued with a video screening of an Encyclopedia Britannica film on mayflies, featuring spectacular close-ups of pulsating *Hexagenia* nymphs.

The students—almost all of them male and outfitted in a variety of T-shirts, ball caps, blue jeans, and shorts—broke for a fly tying session. They set up vises and spread out their materials on three large tables. Humphreys demonstrated tying a sulphur nymph and then turned the students loose on the same pattern. Moving around the room, he kibitzed freely while responding to student questions.

"Hey Joe—I'm having trouble with my tinsel here."

"Hey Humph—what do I do next, put on the tail?"

With mock innocence, another inquired if, on an upcoming trip to Bald Eagle Creek, it would be OK for him to fish with bait.

"Did you hear that?" Humphreys asked the class incredulously. "You're a fly fisherman," he told the student, "and you'll fish only flies."

Not one for political correctness, at one point Humphreys drew the male students' attention to the sea of coeds sunbathing on the lawn outside, and during the movie he compared the undulations of *Hexagenia* nymphs to Gypsy Rose Lee, a reference undoubtedly lost on them.

One of the three girls in the class, a junior biology major from Shippensburg named Cindy Miller, was easily the best flytier in the class, and Humphreys made a point of singling out the quality of her finished sulphur nymph. "We've got lots of good limestone streams where I live," Cindy told me later. "As a kid I grew up fishing bait and spinning. Last spring my father began teaching me fly-fishing. Now that I'm taking this course, I've begun teaching him."

As busy as Humphreys was with his Penn State angling and casting classes, they represented just one aspect of a life devoted to fly-fishing. He had five slide shows on angling techniques and traveled more than he might have wished on the lecture circuit. He made instructional videos and hosted a series on fly-fishing for ESPN, the sports cable network.

Finally, there was fishing itself. Although he didn't keep records, Humphreys figured he got out on a stream at least two hundred days a year. There were regular visits to Montana and to the Great Lakes for their steelhead runs, as well as occasional forays to eastern Canada for Atlantic salmon.

While enjoying the variety of such trips, Humphreys told me, he could fish happily ever after if he were restricted to streams within ten miles of his home. That would encompass some of the most productive and demanding trout waters in eastern North America, including the Little Juniata River and Spruce, Spring, Penns, and Big Fishing Creeks. "If you can solve an angling problem here," he declared, "you can solve one anywhere in the world."

When he wanted good fishing, Humphreys could find it literally in his own backyard. He and his wife, Gloria, lived near the town of Oak Hall on the banks of Spring Creek, a small limestoner descending in a series of stepped pools past their house, a converted gristmill dating from 1822. After a day's teaching, Humphreys said, "I can come home, grab my fly rod, hit a double haul, and be on the stream."

He referred to Spring Creek as his "laboratory," for it was there that he conducted much of the research for his book, *Joe Humphreys's Trout Tactics*. His methodology included donning scuba gear to observe the different ways artificial nymphs drift according to how they are weighted. He found, for example, that with regular-length hooks, wrapping lead wire around the front third of the shank causes them to drift head up (rather than down, as might be supposed), while weighting the center makes the fly turn over and drift upside down. This, of course, would have an important bearing in imitating the action of live nymphs. "Some 98 percent of mayfly nymphs come to the surface head up," Humphreys observes. "For most imitations, therefore, it's not a bad idea to weight the upper third of the shank."

*Trout Tactics* reflects Humphreys's Pennsylvania angling roots and his thoroughly practical approach to finding and catching fish. There are chapters on the importance of water temperature and how geographical features influence temperature; on fishing nymphs, wet flies, streamers, and dries; on brush fishing in small tributaries; and on Humphreys's particular specialty, night fishing for big trout.

"I've been night fishing ever since I was a boy and learned to understand the game fairly well," he said, "and as a schoolteacher I've always had my summers off, so I could stay up most of the night and sleep till noon the next day."

For a period, he recalled, "I got so I wouldn't even go on a stream till it got dark. The darker the better. The insects are flying, the air temperature is warm, the water temperature is cold, it's real nice. Night after night after night. You get to know the water so well. You learn where the big trout lie and that, whenever you take a big fish, another one moves into the same spot to replace it. Big trout always seek colder water, a deeper hole or underwater spring, so you look for a nice cold seep and a velocity change—a perfect lie.

"Once you figure out where the big fish are," he added, "you work on technique. On some nights you can fish big wet-flies near the surface, but if they're not coming up then you have to go down for them with weighted nymphs. Sometimes slow bouncing rolls along the bottom work best; other times you can just let the fly hang there in the current. There's just as much technique in fishing at night as during the day, except you do it all by feel."

Humphreys's obsession with nocturnal angling had paid off in a big way one summer night nine years before. The results of that night are depicted on the cover of *Trout Tactics*—a photograph of Humphreys standing ankle deep in a stream, bending over, and grasping the neck of a staggeringly large fish. Man and monster are surrounded by darkness and illuminated in the camera's electronic flash. On second glance the fish assumes the familiar properties of a heavily spotted brown trout, although one of breathtaking proportions.

The trout, the largest ever caught in Pennsylvania, weighed in at better than fifteen pounds and was two inches shy of a yard long—"a railroad tie with spots," in Humphreys's words. A fish of this size suggests big, open water—the ocean or at least a large lake. Yet Humphreys took it on a stream (Big Fishing Creek) that at its widest is probably no more than sixty feet across. He had stalked this fish for three years before finally catching it in the early hours of August 8, 1977. During all that time, he recalled, "I only saw him once, but sometimes you could hear him feeding—he dined on suckers and small trout, and when he'd go after another fish it sounded like a deer hitting the water. I told myself, 'If you want a record, there he is.'" When Humphreys brought the fish home and put it on the kitchen scales, it weighed 16.6 pounds. "Later I took him to the A&P. It was still the wee hours of the morning, and they were loading the shelves. They had certified scales there, and he came in at 15.5 pounds; somewhere he'd lost a little better than a pound in the five and a half hours since I'd caught him." Fisheries biologists later estimated that the trout was between nine and eleven years old and had spent the first four years of its existence in a hatchery. When planted in the stream it was already between eighteen and twenty inches long—big enough to begin feeding on small fry and eventually on bigger fare. In its years as the stream's resident cannibal, noted Humphreys, "he was responsible for killing a lot of fish."

In his book Humphreys describes catching his Moby Trout in some detail. Like many anglers, however, he is loath to give away all his secrets. A careful reader will notice, for example, that he provides no specifics about the fly pattern used on that memorable night. Later, when I wrote him asking about the pattern, he responded by sending me a sample of it, along with the admonition, "Don't photograph the fly." I didn't. Nor will I describe it here in any more detail than discretion allows. Suffice to say that it was tied on a 2/0 salmon hook and was as big and buggy an example of the flytier's art as I have ever seen. When my wife saw it on the kitchen table, she jumped.

On my visit to the Humphreyses, Joe's behemoth brown—stuffed and mounted above a brass plaque engraved with its vital statistics—swam eternally on the wall of his den. It shared space with other mementos, including photographs of Humphreys at streamside with ex-president Jimmy Carter and Federal Reserve Board chairman Paul Volcker, occasional Pennsylvania anglers who have benefited from his expertise. (He gave Carter, whom he described as "a nice fisherman," his first nymphing lesson, and he helped Volcker with his casting.)

Although proud of his reputation as an angler and a teacher, Humphreys was not one to linger on past accomplishments or associations. He believed he had barely scratched the surface of all he could know about fly-fishing, and he hoped to retire in another year or so to devote himself full-time to further advancing his knowledge. "I've got a hell of a lot more fishing I want to do. I feel the same way as George Harvey, who before he retired used to say how he wanted to stop teaching so he could really start learning about fishing."

His relationship with Harvey, who at the time was in his mid-seventies, recalled other notable friendships in angling history. Like Walton and Cotton or Marinaro and Fox, Humphreys and Harvey shared, after years of fishing and learning together, a deep empathy with each other and their sport. Their friendship was testimony, if any be needed, that there is more to fishing than the mere catching of fish.

Of all the episodes in his ESPN fly-fishing series, Humphreys said he related most personally to one of him and Harvey together on Armstrong Spring Creek in Montana. Gushing full-blown from its limestone bed and running crystal clear to its junction with the Yellowstone, Armstrong is one of the loveliest fishing spots on earth. On that particular morning, its trout were behaving in their usual discriminating manner. After trying and failing with dry flies, Humphreys switched to a tiny emerger and began to connect. This demanding fishing takes keen eyesight. Harvey, who in recent years had undergone cataract surgery, struggled while his former student hooked, landed, and released fish after fish.

Later, when they critiqued the morning, Joe admitted that he had had "a little bit of luck," but he attributed his success to having had "the best fisherman in the country to show me how to do it. You taught me to be flexible and how to get good drifts and drag-free floats," he told Harvey.

Most of all, Humphreys added, "You gave me a lifetime of enjoyment."

The sentiment and the mountain-rimmed setting put Harvey in a reflective mood. "I'm getting to an age now where I don't know how much longer I'm going to be able to get out here and flail this fly around," he said, clearing his throat. "When I climb that mountain and go down the other side, I hope that the journey down will be as pleasant as the one up. And when I reach those pearly gates, I hope that the good Lord feels well enough toward me to stick me in his landing net."

"And release you!"

"Yeah!"

A bit self-consciously, they both laughed. "Shall we catch one more, George?" Humphreys asked.

"Well, I hate to quit. Let's try one more."

## TEN

*Bill Yellowtail:*
*A Crow on*
*the Bighorn*

In May 1990, when I tried to contact Bill Yellowtail about fishing on the Bighorn River, I learned that I couldn't reach him by phone—he didn't have one, even though he was a Montana state senator. That August, when I met him outside the Bighorn Trout Shop in Fort Smith, Montana, I was struck by his size (6 feet 3 and 250 pounds) and a friendliness that was exceptional even by western standards. Later, as I thought back on the two days I spent with him—one floating the Bighorn, the other roaming his remote ranch in the foothills of the Bighorn Mountains—what stuck in my mind was his laugh. As sunny as a prairie morning, it punctuated his remarks on a variety of subjects that concerned him, from the status of the Bighorn fishery (great but could be greater, in his view) to his legislative efforts on behalf of small ranchers, sportsmen, and the environment.

Along with ranching and politicking, Yellowtail occasionally guided on the thirteen-mile blue-ribbon stretch of the Bighorn below Yellowtail Dam (named for great-uncle Bob, the chairman of the Crow tribal council when the dam was built in the early 1960s). Flowing at a cool, constant temperature and boasting a high pH from its limestone substrate, the water issuing from the bottom of the dam is the source of the Bighorn's status as one of the best trout fisheries on earth. Fertile weed beds support a dense population of scuds and aquatic insects, the food base for nearly 10,000 wild trout per mile.

Although I had read for years about the Bighorn, this was my introduction to it and Bill Yellowtail would be doing the honors. Admittedly there were plenty of full-time guides who, being on the river daily, were more current on how it was fishing. By contrast, the demands of the family ranch limited Yellowtail's guiding and personal fishing, so he was lucky to get on the Bighorn once every couple of weeks. But his knowledge of the river and its watershed ran deep and amounted to a kind of birthright. His people, the Crow, had been living in these parts for three centuries. He had grown up in the Bighorn Mountains and knew the river from its days as a warm-water fishery. He had fly-fished on it for more than twenty years.

I had learned about Yellowtail from a profile of him by Perri Knize in *Audubon* magazine, a piece that focused on his environmental work in the state senate. After Silvio Calabi, the editor of *Fly Rod & Reel,* gave me a go-ahead to do a story about him, I called Off the Beaten Path, a Bozeman-based travel agency that handled his bookings. Its receptionist said she'd heard that Yellowtail had recently installed a phone and I might be able to talk to him directly, but my hopes were dashed in a subsequent call from Bill Bryan, the agency's founder. "Any rumors you may have heard about Bill getting a phone are false," he said. "First of all, it would cost him an arm and a leg to run a wire out to his place. And frankly, he doesn't want to be bothered by calls. There's a phone twenty-five miles from his place, and when he needs to make a call, he drives there."

Because some fishing writers follow the questionable practice of negotiating free trips from guides in exchange for publicity, I felt obliged to emphasize that I would, of course, pay Yellowtail for his services. "If you could do that, that's great," said Bryan. "He has no sense of money. If a writer asked to float the Bighorn with him, he might say, 'Aw shucks, let's go ahead,' without asking or even thinking about payment. But the $200 you give him—he needs it!"

Bryan arranged for me to meet Bill at Fort Smith, the sleepy trailer-park town at the base of Yellowtail Dam. Three months later, my wife, Nancy, and I found ourselves standing outside the Bighorn Trout Shop when Bill Yellowtail pulled up in a cloud of dust in a van, hauling a drift boat.

It was a short drive to the Afterbay Access, where, to keep the river level constant, a smaller dam holds back surges of water released from the big dam for power generation. Crow warriors—Yellowtail's ancestors—had once camped along this part of the river when, during Red Cloud's War, they had fought as allies of the U.S. Army against their traditional enemies, the Sioux. The old Bozeman Trail, the route to the Montana gold fields that had sparked that conflict, had crossed the Bighorn at this very spot. A century and a quarter before, wagons filled with men and supplies bound for the boom towns of Bannack and Virginia City had forded the river here; now fiberglass boats carrying anglers in neoprene waders jockeyed for position. With a grin, Bill heaved on the oars as we began our descent of the river.

The Bighorn's clarity and beauty astonished me. The river flows transparent over a bottom of undulant weeds and past groves of cottonwoods that give its banks an almost park-like appearance. It has the character and prolific hatches of a giant spring creek, and Bill expected a good hatch of Pale Morning Duns to come off later in the day. In the meantime, we worked a white caddis pupa imitation that picked up two small trout at the Suck Hole (also called "the Concrete"), a pool formed by the remains of an old irrigation dam. A little farther down, we parked the boat to wade the head of a riffle. On the fourth or fifth cast, my strike indicator surged and I was into a thick brown of sixteen inches. We marveled at the deep color of its crimson flanks. His big frame hunched over the fish, Yellowtail tipped back his cap and laughed.

"Will you look at that Bighorn brown!" he exclaimed, as though seeing one for the first time. "Is that OK? I love it!"

Perhaps because of the brightness of the day, the Pale Morning Duns were failing to live up to their name, but once they began showing in midafternoon it was like someone had flipped a switch. Suddenly, surface-feeding trout seemed to be everywhere. The fishing wasn't easy, requiring close imitation and leaders tapering to 5X and 6X. In frustration, I watched as trout after trout ignored my fly or inspected it briefly before refusing—typical behavior, Bill noted ruefully. "I've fished some of these pools for hours, cursing the fish the whole time. Slurp, slurp, slurp—have you ever heard a trout laugh derisively? That's what it sounds like."

With persistent casting we picked up more fish, and by the time we left the river our tally stood at a dozen browns hooked and ten landed, all but two between sixteen and nineteen inches. Yellowtail pronounced the day "better than average" for the Bighorn, adding bonus points for the relatively few anglers we encountered. Although never out of sight of other boats, we were usually separated from them by a hundred yards or better. We were about a week ahead of the August-September crunch, when a succession of hatches draws a vast flotilla and brings out the worst in some fishermen. "This place can really go nuts," Bill said. "I haven't seen any fisticuffs yet, but I've witnessed some real shouting matches. Some of them got pretty ugly. A few people have got terrible manners, they'll run right over your fishing. The guides try really hard to be considerate, but sometimes there are just too many fishermen."

Like many of the Bighorn's fly-fishing regulars, Yellowtail believed it suffered from so much pressure, and he hoped to see more restrictive regulations placed upon it. At the time, the Bighorn's prime thirteen-mile stretch had no closed season, and an angler could keep five browns per day. Among Yellowtail's prescriptions: imposing a slot limit, which would allow anglers to keep only the smallest and very biggest fish; closing the river in the spring, when rainbows (outnumbered by browns nine-to-one) are spawning; and—the change least likely to be implemented—imposing a permit system to control crowding. "This river is a national treasure," he said, "and ought to be managed accordingly."

Yellowtail's affair with the Bighorn went back to childhood. He recalled sitting on the rocks high above it, where the five-hundred-foot-high Yellowtail Dam now stands, watching the river spill out of Bighorn Canyon onto the plains. He remembered his grandfather netting catfish and other warmwater species before the dam (a creation of the Bureau of Reclamation) turned the river into a trout fishery overnight. Despite his passion for fly-fishing, Yellowtail regarded the dam with ambivalence, for the canyon it flooded was an important wintering ground for elk and held spiritual significance for the

Crow. The construction, in the early 1960s, was opposed by the tribal council, but the feds went ahead anyway, condemning the land and paying off the tribe. As Yellowtail recalled, "All of us got something like $2,000 each out of the deal—we went to town and bought a car and a new pair of boots and that was it."

Upon completion of the dam, the Bighorn rapidly earned its reputation as a premier trout river. Angered by the legions of fishermen invading their reservation, the tribal council closed the river in 1976, and for the next six years only Crow could fish it. "You wouldn't believe how good it was," Bill recalled. White fishermen sued over the matter, and in 1982 the U.S. Supreme Court reopened the river to all comers.

Yellowtail said he was disappointed that few Crow benefited economically from the fishery; shop owners and guides who made their livings off the river were virtually all Anglos. He attributed this to a lack of entrepreneurial tradition among the Crow and to their lingering resentment over the dam's construction. After the Crow blocked access to the river, Bill said, he urged the tribal council to allow fishing on a fee basis, something that other tribes—including the Northern Cheyenne, who charge anglers to fish on the Wind River, a Bighorn tributary—had done on their waters. But nothing had come of the idea, and on the Bighorn's blue-ribbon stretch, at least, Crow remained conspicuous by their absence.

Bill Yellowtail learned fly-fishing from his father, a rancher who by reservation standards was relatively prosperous. He fished Lodge Grass Creek, a pretty little stream that cuts through the Chugwater sandstone of the Bighorn foothills, where Yellowtails have ranched for three generations. "He was deadly," Bill said. "And of course, he didn't believe in turning them loose. I used to follow him around with my worm, but he seemed to be having so much fun with a fly rod that I decided to try it myself."

The senior Yellowtail made it clear to his three sons and daughter (Bill is the eldest) that they would go to college. A star student and athlete at Lodge Grass High School, Bill thought it would be "adventuresome" to attend Eastern Montana College in nearby Billings. Instead, his father insisted that he apply to Harvard and Dartmouth; his lawyer had a degree from the former and his car dealer had a son at the latter. "I'd never even heard of Dartmouth—it sounded like a cattle disease to me," Bill recalled. Both schools accepted him, and he picked Dartmouth on the basis of the literature sent him by its outdoor club. "Some sense told me that I might not survive well in Boston. I've been there since, and that was one of the few good decisions I've ever made."

The Yellowtail ranch was miles from the nearest town, with no running water and no telephone. Electricity came from a generator, at least when it worked. Except for a glance at Denver during a family trip, Bill had never seen a city bigger than Billings, and he had never been on an airplane. "Two days before leaving for college, we were still at cow camp up in the mountains, where we kept our cattle for the summer. I remember saddling my horse and riding home with real trepidation."

He barely survived his Ivy League education. The sole Indian at Dartmouth (his arrival preceded by several years the school's efforts to recruit Native Americans), he was desperately homesick and overwhelmed by the academics. In an act of desperation that years later he was still at a loss to explain, he was caught breaking into a camera store. Dartmouth suspended him. For the next two years he worked on the ranch and studied at Montana State University, in Bozeman; after reenrolling at Dartmouth, he graduated in 1971 with honors in geography and then stayed on for two years to recruit and counsel Native American students. He then returned home, married a Sioux, and worked for the Crow tribal council as director of education. (Revelations about the breaking and entering, as well as other problems of his youth, would dog Yellowtail in 1996, when, as a Democrat, he ran unsuccessfully for Montana's single congressional seat. During the campaign, newspapers reported both the burglary and Yellowtail's past marital problems: in the heat of an argument with his first wife he had struck her, and after their divorce he had reneged on child payments to support their daughter. "If I had my druthers," he told the press, "I'd take all those things back in a second.")

After his father's death in 1981, Bill helped operate the family ranch with his mother, Jane, and brother Carson. At the time of my visit, the Yellowtails owned 7,000 acres, leased another 13,000, and ran 500 head of cattle. "We once dabbled in sheep—it made the coyotes and bears real happy for a couple of years," he said.

In 1984, Montana Democrats asked Yellowtail to run for the state senate from the Fiftieth District, whose borders had recently been redrawn to include the entire Crow and Northern Cheyenne reservations, making an Indian victory feasible. He won in a squeaker, becoming the first Native American to serve in Montana's upper house, and four years later was handily re-elected. An environmental advocate, he sat on the senate fish and game committee and the state's new Environmental Quality Council. His district stretched from Pryor Creek to the Powder River, covering an area the size of New Jersey; its population of 15,000, said Yellowtail, was 40 percent Indian but also included "ranchers, coal miners, all types—and they don't always agree."

The Montana legislature meets once every two years for a three-month session. When Yellowtail arrived in Helena for his first session (carrying his clothes in a plastic garbage bag), he landed in the middle of a political firestorm over the issue of stream access. Several years earlier, a property owner on the Beaverhead had strung wire across the river, blocking drift boats. The inevitable lawsuit followed, resulting in a decision by the state supreme court declaring that if a fisherman gained legal access to a stream (for example, by launching a boat on public property), private landowners along the stream could not restrict his use of it.

"The whole stream-access controversy came to a head," Yellowtail recalled. "The court had ruled on the principle of stream right-of-way but left the details of interpreting the principle up to the legislature. I was pretty naive and was talked into sponsoring the bill that eventually became the law. There were all kinds of questions we had to deal with. For example, should you be permitted to camp on a stream? Should shooting be permitted? Ranchers wanted a highly restrictive law, but I felt that the legislation had to honor the court's mandate. We held hearings that packed the halls with angry ranchers on one side and angry recreationists on the other. It took the entire session to get the bill through the legislature. We wound up establishing a strict classification system for streams and what was permissible on them. The law also allows landowners to petition the state for stream closure under specific circumstances, but a lot of ranchers are still unhappy, including many in my district."

He regained some favor among his ranching constituency by sponsoring legislation granting relief to small ranches facing foreclosure in tough economic times. Reeling from depressed beef prices and a decade of drought, family ranches were disappearing in Montana at a rate of twenty-eight per week. Typically, said Yellowtail, "the banks will foreclose, then write off the first million dollars of debt and sell the property to some corporation in Utah. Why can't they give the same break to the original owners? I've watched hundreds of old family operations go belly-up. It's a real tragedy, not only for the economy but for the fabric of the community."

His populist sentiments stemmed from personal experience, for the Yellowtails themselves had barely survived the ruthless economics of small-scale ranching. Four years earlier, they almost lost their place after the bank holding their notes went under. The FDIC demanded immediate payment, forcing them to sell off every head of cattle. Bill told me that their hold on the land remained tenuous. A wealthy oilman from Salt Lake City had bought all the property around them and was now eyeing the Yellowtail spread. Small ranchers, Bill said, "view property on its productive capacity. Our valley is worth what it will return to us in cows or hay. But Montana is a bargain for outsiders. They come in and impose a different value system, and it becomes very tempting to sell out."

You can see this happening on the Bighorn, he added. "Riverfront property is going for $2,000 an acre. That's impossible for us, but for a group of Denver doctors who want to build a weekend place, it's a pittance. Without proper zoning—something woefully lacking throughout Montana—it's only a matter of time before we'll have condos on the river."

After our long day on the Bighorn, Nancy and I followed Yellowtail to his ranch in the mountains. The last part of the hour-and-a-half drive was over gravel and dirt. The dust kicked up by Bill's van swirled in the headlights of our car. Bouncing and bucking over the rutted road, I was convinced that National Car Rental would never do business with me again.

The next morning, I crawled out of our tent and joined Bill in the kitchen of his mother's three-room log cabin. A spry, angular woman in her late sixties, Jane Yellowtail served us a breakfast of fried eggs, bacon, and pancakes soaked in homemade chokeberry syrup. When I told her I had slept well, she feigned surprise. "No rattlesnakes in your bed? No bears? What a disappointing night!" The day before, she'd killed a rattler in the yard, and the previous winter a hungry bear had tried to break into the house. "You can still see his tracks on the window," Bill said.

Jane, I learned, was of Scotch-Irish descent and had met Bill's father when he worked on her family's ranch in the

1940s. After they eloped, her father disowned her for marrying an Indian. The home in which Jane raised Bill and his two brothers and sister now boasted a few amenities it lacked when they were growing up. The utility company ran a wire out to the place around 1970, and in the late 1980s Bill and Carson installed plumbing. Otherwise, the ranch remained as primitive and isolated as it had been when Bill was born forty-two years before. The nearest town, Wyola (population sixty), was more than twenty miles away, noted Bill, but after a big snowstorm it "might as well be 20,000 miles. We're blessed with Chinook winds, which can evaporate snow in a day. But there are times when you can't get out of here for two weeks. We keep a good supply of groceries on hand."

Bill and his second wife, Maggie (who during our stay was visiting her folks in Oregon), lived in a trailer a short walk from the cabin. A sculptor whom Bill met in 1979 when she came to the reservation on a grant from the National Endowment for the Humanities, she was teaching at the high school in Lodge Grass, forty miles away, spending the week there while school was in session.

By materialistic standards the Yellowtails' way of life was Spartan. In a typical year, they were lucky to clear $10,000 from ranching. Bill supplemented this by guiding on the Bighorn and occasionally leading tours of the Custer (now Little Bighorn) Battlefield and Montana's Indian reservations for Off the Beaten Path. The state paid him $100 a day when the legislature was in session—"If I'm real careful, I don't lose money," he said.

After breakfast, we explored part of the ranch in Bill's old green Ford pickup (no brakes but a good transmission). When we paused on a bluff to look at some ancient tipi rings, Bill said, "Not too far from here we've got what I'm certain was a buffalo jump. It's actually two spots, one where the Indians slaughtered the buffalo, another where they butchered them." He motioned to some distant timbered slopes. "Do you see that notch in the mountains? Just beyond it is where we had our cow camp. Our family would spend the entire summer up there, camped out, working the cattle, each of us kids with his own horse. It was wonderful . . ."

Below us, Lodge Grass Creek, where his dad had taught him fly-fishing—"a debilitating disease," Bill called it, although it was one he suffered gladly—wound its way down the valley toward the Little Bighorn. I recalled our day on the Bighorn itself, drifting at dusk on its glassy, backlit currents through shoals of rising trout feeding on spinners, and the joy in his voice at the sight. "Boy," he said. "Are we lucky out here!"

## ELEVEN

# "This Old Guy Named Waterman"

"Charley Waterman is alive and well and living in De Land, Florida, and Livingston, Montana."

It was about four years before I wrote these words that I called Silvio Calabi, the editor of *Fly Rod & Reel,* asking him if he would like me to profile Waterman, one of the deans of American outdoor writers and a man whose fly-fishing spanned seven decades.

"You're too late," said Silvio. "He just died."

"Damn! You must be kidding."

"Nope. Happened just a few weeks ago."

My only contact with Waterman had been a brief telephone conversation a year before, when I interviewed him for my profile of Dan Bailey. Having gained a sense of his wry personality and self-deprecating humor from his pieces in *Gray's Sporting Journal* and other publications, I was disappointed that I would never have the opportunity to meet him.

It seemed odd that I saw no obituaries in any of the magazines Waterman wrote for, and odder still when articles kept appearing under his byline. At first I assumed the magazines were just cleaning out their story banks. When I called Silvio again and reminded him of what he'd told me about Waterman's demise, he sounded genuinely surprised.

"I said that? Gee, I must have been confusing him with someone else." (I later figured out that he had gotten Charley Waterman confused with Charlie Brooks, a well-known Montana angling author, who in fact had just died.)

In the summer of 1989, when I finally met Charley Waterman at his home in Livingston, I didn't tell him this story. It is vintage Waterman, the kind of anecdote he can't resist telling on himself, and I didn't want him to get into print with it before me.

Charley and Debie Waterman were living with their two dogs—a Brittany spaniel named Spike and an English pointer who answered to Dutch (after the Duchess of Doonesbury)—in a three-room bungalow on the edge of town. It was an unpretentious place, in keeping with the character of Uncle Charley himself, whom John Randolph, the editor of *Fly Fisherman,* had described to me as "a writer without an ego"—about as rare a creature as a trout without spots.

Waterman's easy manner and gentle midwestern drawl were just what I had come to expect from his writing. He looked and talked a decade younger than his actual age (he was in his mid-seventies), the result, no doubt, of a life spent in the outdoors, doing exactly what he wanted and answering to no man but himself. Raised on a farm in Kansas, Waterman had been fishing and hunting more or less continuously since 1920, and for the last forty years he had managed to make a modest but sufficient living by writing about the sports he loved. In addition to being one of the most prolific outdoor scribes in the business—he has written for scores of magazines and at that juncture in his career was the author of fourteen books—at various times he has also been a schoolteacher, a newspaper reporter, a combat photographer, a private detective, and a semipro wrestler. Our conversation touched on all these topics and more.

At Silvio's suggestion, I wrote the piece in a question-and-answer format rather than a narrative.

*Let's start from the beginning. In your two autobiographical books—*The Part I Remember *and* Times and Places, Home and Away*—you write about what must have been an idyllic childhood, growing up on a Kansas farm.*

I was born in Girard, Kansas, in the southeastern part of the state. It's rolling country there, with more diversified farming than you find farther west, and with smaller farms—most of them the original 160-acre land grants. Farmers like my dad were pretty self-sufficient. They'd farm twenty acres of wheat, twenty acres of oats, forty of corn—we shucked corn by hand. Then we had chickens, turkeys, and milk and beef cattle. A farmer wouldn't starve, but he wouldn't get rich, either.

*What was the hunting and fishing like?*

We didn't have deer in Kansas at the time, but there were plenty of quail and rabbit, and bass in the tank ponds—these were impoundments made from damming up a creek where a railroad crossed it, so the steam locomotives could take on water. During summer you could wade them wet, fishing hair and popping bugs. I had a cheap bamboo fly rod I bought for $2 and rigged with a bait-casting line. Some of the regulars fished those tank ponds floating in an old truck inner tube rigged with a harness; it amuses me today to read about things of supposedly recent origin, like belly boats, which I first saw back in the 1920s.

At home I fished the tank ponds, but the Ozarks weren't far away. We had a Model T Ford, and by age fourteen or so I was driving down there to camp and fish for smallmouth on the James and White Rivers. I really lost my head over the Ozarks—it was hard to keep me away.

*You obviously liked the Midwest, because it was a long time before you left.*

I went to State Teacher's College in Pittsburg, Kansas. I studied English and speech but wasn't much of a student. Then I taught grade school briefly before going to work for the Pittsburg *Headlight* at $15 per week. I was a general-assignment reporter—not a very good one—driving around the coal towns, picking up odds and ends.

It was while I was teaching school that I moonlighted as a semipro wrestler, working the weekend carnival circuits in Kansas and Oklahoma for $5 a match. I weighed about 165 pounds but might be listed at 190, which was stretching it a bit. The matches were rehearsed, although not exactly rigged the way they are today. We had heroes and villains—or "wrestlers" and "heels" as we called them—but without the fancy costumes and clowning. I went by the name of Charley Redd, and with my kid's face and blond hair, I made a pretty fair "wrestler."

It wasn't until World War II that I saw anything else of the world. I'd done newspaper photography, so I signed up with the navy as a photographer's mate. Later I got a commission and wound up with one of Edward Steichen's photo teams in the South Pacific. I was old enough to have stayed out of the service, but I just couldn't do it. I wasn't at all adventuresome, but this was the biggest thing of our time, and I didn't want to spend it at home writing about Rotary meetings. And if it hadn't been for the war I'd never have hooked up with Debie. I was teaching photography at Pensacola, Florida, and met her in West Palm Beach. She was running a restaurant there, and it didn't take long before we discovered our mutual interest. Debie had grown up in a Michigan family of outdoorsmen and was a real fishing nut.

*Were you doing any outdoor writing then?*

Not during the war, although I'd been thinking about it for a long time. I was seven years old when I decided to become an outdoor writer. We had a 1914 copy of the old *National Sportsman* around the house—I still have the magazine—and it had a fishing story by Newton Newkirk that got me thinking about the possibilities. As a reporter I wrote an outdoor column on the side, although the editors thought I was wasting my time.

After the war, Debie and I moved to San Mateo, California, where she worked as a corsetiere and I became a freelance photographer, fishing and hunting whenever I could. When Debie found a job in Denver, I followed her there and worked for a detective agency. I became a whiz at surveillance and had a surefire system for following people without being detected. I simply dressed in clothes the subject would never wear. If following a banker, I dressed like a workman, complete with dinner pail. If my subject worked with his hands, I dressed like a businessman, carrying a briefcase.

It wasn't until the early 1950s, about the time we left Denver for Florida, that I cut loose and decided to try full-time outdoor writing. People who knew anything about the business told me I was crazy—the few people writing the stuff regularly, like Ray Bergman and Al McClane, were on magazine staffs, not freelancing like I planned to do. I sold my first free-lance article—a piece on fishing the North Platte in Wyoming—to *Fisherman* magazine, which was published in Ohio. It eventually went broke. A lot of magazines I've written for have done that, and most of them have owed me money at one time or another. It was touch-and-go for a long time, and I must have been fifty years old before I felt secure in the field. It helped not having children. If I'd had a family to support, I don't see how we could have done the things we have.

*What magazines do you write for now? And what's your writing routine?*

I think there are seven in all that I contribute to on a regular basis. Let's see if I can just list them. There's *Gray's, Gun Dog, Wing and Shot, Florida Sportsman, Salt Water Sportsman* . . . two to go. Oh yeah—*Fishing World,* plus a new quarterly whose name escapes me right now. I've written for the bigger ones too, like *Field & Stream* and *Outdoor Life,* although not for a while. The midsize magazines don't pay as much—I probably average about $400 a story—but you get enough of them lined up and it brings in the groceries.

A lot of writers complain about writing, but I've never thought of it as a chore. I'd just as soon write as fish. I don't have any set routine and can do it at night, in the morning, whenever—I could go in there right now and bang out a column as easily as if I'd primed myself for it all day. I don't think of myself as being especially creative—most of it's just nuts and bolts, with a personal touch. I try to keep it simple. I have a rule that I won't write anything a fifth grader can't understand if he applies himself. I don't pose as an authority, although strangely people tend to accept me as one.

The computer—word processing—has really saved my bacon. I use an IBM PC in Florida and a Sylvania portable here in Montana. My software is Writer's Assistant. I keep a disk for each magazine and can do 2,000 words in a little more than half a day. The thing that's hardest is trying to remember which anecdotes I've used before. Poor Debie has to read everything to make sure I'm not repeating myself.

*When talking about your work, you say "we" as much as "I"—referring, obviously, to Debie. And from the credits on the pictures with your articles, it seems she takes most of the photographs.*

If there's a close-up of a person in one of our shots, it's usually of me and taken by Debie. If the subject is in the middle distance and can't be identified, it's usually Debie and I'm the photographer. We have a whole pile of hats and clothes, and to lend variety to our pictures we change them all the time. In the pictures of Debie, she's usually looking away, and you can't tell it's a woman. This is deliberate. Sex is great, but forget it in hunting or fishing. Men are the main readers of outdoor magazines, and I'm convinced they don't want to see any picture of a woman fishing, especially if it's a woman over thirty.

*Speaking of pictures, you wrote once about faking those spectacular shots of leaping fish, the ones that editors think sell their magazines.*

It may be less true today, but for years editors demanded those dramatic jump shots for their covers. There are different techniques for getting them, but I always preferred the cement-block method. You get this cement block with a loop of rope tied around it and drop it into shoulder-deep water. Then you get in the water and hook your foot into the loop, which keeps you anchored. The photographer is in the boat a few feet away. You hold the fish just below the surface and on a signal throw it into the air while dunking yourself. The fish carries water with it, while the splash you make looks like the fish exploding from the surface.

*You've been fly-fishing for better than sixty years. How have you seen the sport change?*

That's a big question. I suppose the biggest change is on the technical side, in addition to much better casting and knowledge of entomology. There's a higher level of learning. And of course the sport has become a lot more popular, with many people taking it up because it's the thing to do, although I'm not sure how many stay with it.

Another thing that has changed is the acceptance, at least among fly fishermen, of the catch-and-release philosophy. It's even begun to spread to other kinds of fishing, although there are people who resent it, and fly fishing in general. I remember once, wading the St. John's River in Florida during the shad run, fishing with a fly rod and watching a steady parade of trollers who didn't realize that what they were saying about me carried some distance on the water. The gist of their remarks was that people like me thought they were better than others. By and large, fly fishermen do think they're better, although I'm not sure it's at all justified.

*You and Debie enjoy an enviable lifestyle. How much do you get to hunt and fish, and how do you divide your time between Florida and Montana?*

My standard answer to the first part of your question is two hundred days a year—if you're going to write about this stuff, you've got to do it! As for the second part, we generally drive up here in early July—we haul the dogs with us—and stay until the first part of December. The fishing's at its peak then, and the bird hunting for grouse and Hungarian partridge is real good in the fall. The dogs are getting on in years—Spike is almost eleven and Dutch twelve—and once they get too old to work birds, I may retire from hunting too.

We've been coming to Livingston since 1957, when Joe Brooks, the late outdoor writer and our good friend, told us about the great fishing here. We like the spring creeks especially, although neither one of us is a highly technical fisherman, and we're pretty lax on the Latin. We're not good nymph fishermen and prefer dries. Debie ties our flies. Her best are a couple of little things in sizes twenty and twenty-two. She calls them the Teeny Weeny and the Hangy Downy. We don't know what they match and they wouldn't meet commercial standards, but they do catch fish.

Debie is an excellent fisherman, and there are things she does a lot better than I do. We used to do a lot of plug casting for snook in the Everglades, and she always caught bigger fish. I finally figured out why. Like most men, I always jerked the plug hard; but she retrieved it more gently and that's what the big snook liked.

Debie was also the first woman to land a stream-caught fish for "the wall" at Dan Bailey's Fly Shop here. Back in the fifties and sixties especially, people used to come out to Livingston for the sole purpose of catching a fish four pounds or bigger so they could get its outline on the wall at Bailey's. Debie got up there several years ahead of me with a big brown from the Yellowstone, and I took quite a bit of ribbing about it. At the Murray Hotel coffee shop people used to point me out as the man whose wife had caught a wall fish.

*Of the many kinds of fishing you've done, what's your favorite?*

I have to be careful about this, but if restricted to just one type of fishing, I guess it would be the spring-creek fly-fishing. My second choice would be fly-fishing for snook in brackish water. It's rather coarse fishing, with none of the mystique, say, of tarpon, but these are big fish—up to ten and twelve pounds—and great fun when caught on a long streamer or an outsized bass bug. For years I made a specialty of fishing shoreline spots in the Everglades for them. I knew all the best places. I didn't realize what a veteran I'd become until one time when I found a guy in a fancy bass boat fishing one of my favorite spots. I had no lease on the place so I cranked up and went to another miles away, but within fifteen minutes the same guy showed up there.

When I idled over and inquired how he could know two of my pet places, he told me he had a chart marked with all the best snook spots. "I got it from so-and-so, and he got his chart marked by so-and-so before he died, who got his marked by this old guy named Waterman, who used to fish down here."

## TWELVE

*Going for Broke:*
*Filmmakers*
*Jim and Kelly*
*Watt*

A year after my float with Bill Yellowtail I was back on the Bighorn, again on assignment for *Fly Rod & Reel*. This time I was fishing with Jim and Kelly Watt, the producers of *Fly Fishing Video Magazine*. It was late August, and they were midway through a week of fishing and filming. A month before, the Watts had been fishing for Atlantic salmon on Russia's Kola Peninsula. Before that, they'd been to British Columbia for Kamloops trout, to Florida for tarpon, to Ontario for spring-creek rainbows, to Costa Rica for sailfish and marlin, and to the Yucatan for bonefish. In the months ahead they would be casting for billfish in the Atlantic off Senegal and for trout in the desert lakes of the Pacific Northwest. Then there was the fishing ranch in Chile they planned to explore early in the following year, and a new salmon camp in Siberia. There are worse ways to make a living.

It was the Thursday before Labor Day weekend, the fourth day on the river for the Watts, and they were still looking for some prime footage for their video about the Bighorn. Despite the river's abundance, during the previous three days they had taken fewer than a half dozen fish. Unusually hot weather had made the trout sulky, and they were feeding for only an hour or two in the morning. Our guide, Richie Montella, an ex-New Jerseyan who had fished the Bighorn for a decade and knew the river as well as anyone, shook his head and champed on his ever-present stogie. "This has been *tough* fishing," he said.

To catch what we could of the morning activity, we put into the river at 7:30 A.M., a good two hours earlier than normal for August. While Montella backed his McKenzie boat into the water at the Afterbay Access, just below Yellowtail Dam, Kelly wired me with a remote microphone and a radio transmitter embedded in a Velcro strap, which she slipped under my shirt. Jim parked their van (emblazoned with the company logo) and hung on its side a Plexiglas box filled with promotional brochures, remarking that "the biggest problem we have is people saying they've never heard of us." Then he counted the brochures so that at the end of the day he would know how many potential subscribers had taken one.

A compact, crew-cut man in his late forties, Jim Watt told me he had grown up in Kansas City and had learned to fly-fish for bass and bluegills on farm ponds and in Ozark streams. He went to junior college and briefly attended the University of Missouri. But "they kicked me out because I never went to class." Then he worked as a TV cameraman, initially for a local news operation and later as a freelancer in Vietnam, where he spent a total of fourteen months between 1968 and 1974 (he was there during the Tet Offensive and the fall of Saigon). Restless by nature, he settled for a while into a network job for NBC in Burbank, California, but in 1978 he moved to Seattle and resumed freelancing. "I realized that I could work for all three networks that way and have more time to fish."

Kelly Bennett Watt, a willowy blond in her late twenties, shared her husband's passion for fly-fishing, a sport he introduced her to. As a kid growing up in Bellevue, Washington, she recalled, "I did some fishing with my father, but never fly fishing. He fishes with lures for salmon, and he keeps everything he catches. He still thinks I'm nuts for letting them go." At the University of Washington she played tennis and volleyball, and her athletic abilities are apparent in her powerful casting, which she puts to good use on their saltwater trips. Kelly, Jim told me, had caught more than fifty sailfish on a fly—probably more than any other woman.

I learned more about their backgrounds as we slipped down river ahead of most of the boat traffic. In 1986 Kelly was two years out of college and working as a sound technician for a local TV station when she met Jim during a shoot-out between police and Robert Matthews, a neo-Nazi holed up on an island north of Seattle. (Matthews was incinerated after police torched his hideout—"a whacko . . . converted to a crispy critter," as one newspaper delicately put it.) Despite such an inauspicious start, romance flowered, and the two married later that year, she for the first time, he for the second; Jim had three grown children by a previous marriage.

We floated the Bighorn for about a mile, drifting over a rich carpet of weeds waving in the current while the sun winked through the cottonwoods, warmed the prairie bluffs, and backlit furious clouds of *Tricorythodes* spinners hovering over the river. According to Montella, the Tricos were more than a month ahead of schedule, the result of warm-water releases from the dam, and the spinner falls were as thick as he could remember. It made for demanding fishing, as I discovered after we put into the backwater at the Red Cliffs and waded into position below a pod of gorging fish. Montella and the Watts called these congregations of feeding trout "wolf packs," and the sight of this one was unnerving—perhaps fifty big fish packed into a narrow feeding lane and taking the spent-wing flies in a steady rhythm.

It would have been hard enough to catch these gulpers under normal circumstances, much less with Jim Watt kneeling beside me, camera balanced on his shoulder, capturing my ineptitude on tape. With Montella directing, I spent a fruitless hour casting, switching flies from a spinner pattern to a dun to a Griffith's Gnat and back to the spinner. It was nearly impossible to pick out my fly from the hundreds of naturals on the water, but when Montella yelled "strike!" I did, and after some clumsy line handling—also recorded for posterity—he slipped the net under a glistening eighteen-inch rainbow. Given the selectivity of these fish, I couldn't be too embarrassed about my performance. I took comfort too in Jim's telling me that the typical ratio of footage shot to footage used is about thirty to one, so the chance of this sequence appearing in the video was slight. (I beat the odds; it's in there—along with the cows that came down the bank to drink, spoiling the rest of our fishing.)

The Watts had slotted their volume on the Bighorn for release the following June. Like the six hour-long videos they produced every year, it would follow a predictable format: in this case, there would be an opening segment with Montella discussing the river and how they expected to fish it, followed by action scenes interspersed with segments on fly tying and casting, plus a brief commercial or two (their sponsors included Loomis and 3M) and an "if-you-go" section on transportation and local accommodations. The Watts were the on-air hosts, and their approach to a show was low-key. "We're average fly fishermen, and we tell the guides to treat us like a couple of rubes," said Jim. "The whole concept is that the fish are the stars and guys like Richie are the experts."

Economists will tell you that most small businesses start out undercapitalized. This truism certainly applied to Bennett/Watt Enterprises, the magazine's parent firm (under which the Watts also worked on freelance nonfishing projects, including occasional network assignments and aerobics videos). Prior to launching the magazine in 1987, Jim said, "We went to the banks with a business plan, but they wouldn't lend us a dime—they just laughed." So the Watts borrowed money from a friend, and they had recently taken out a second mortgage on their house to pay for a major marketing campaign, which they hoped would triple their subscription base of 1,000. Jim figured that about $100,000 of the estimated $1 million that had gone into the business since its debut had been financed by their credit cards. "I put myself through school playing poker and gin rummy, so I've always been a gambler," he said. "I think of this as the biggest poker game I've been in."

To make ends meet they kept overhead to a minimum. Bennett/Watt Enterprises had only one other employee (a part-time director of sales and marketing), and all editing and production were done in-house by Jim and Kelly. Sponsors supplied fishing gear, guides and lodges tendered their services free in exchange for the publicity, and whenever possible the Watts cut promotional deals with airlines.

Like many entrepreneurs, Jim Watt began with a vision of what he wanted to do and built the business through trial and error. One mistake made several years before—bringing in a well-heeled partner who agreed to underwrite the magazine on condition that it be broadened to include spin fishing and bait casting, with a concurrent change of title to *Angling Video Magazine*—almost sunk the enterprise, according to Jim. "We lost nearly 30 percent of our subscribers, who wanted only fly-fishing."

The Watts got back on track and had since become more sophisticated about marketing, a subject "we knew nothing about when we started," Jim said. They had put $35,000 into their latest marketing drive and had arranged for resorts and fly shops to display their brochures, with the owners getting a cut on resulting sales. They were reorganizing as a video club with a more flexible price schedule and were shopping for distributors in Europe and Japan and working on a deal to show some of their episodes on cable television. They also did a side business selling back issues. "Any way you can move a few tapes is good," said Jim.

The Watts had $140,000 in camera, sound, and editing equipment to maintain and insure. Remarkably, they had only dunked a camera once, and they went to unusual lengths to protect their gear from the elements. At the end of our last day on the river, Jim told me that to keep moisture out of their radio transmitters they wrap them in condoms. I blushed to learn I'd been wearing one unawares. "It can be hard finding the unlubricated kind," he said. "After we've had them spread out on a table in some Latin American hotel for a few days, the maids just smile at us."

The next morning we were on the water by 6:15. We put in at the Three Mile Access for a short float to the braided riffles above the Snag Hole. Soon the predictable waves of spinners appeared, and we began to spot cruising fish. "Watch those seams and you'll see 'em feeding." said Montella. "Blind casting doesn't do it on this river." It was Kelly's turn to fish, with Jim on the camera. Casting a size-twenty barbless Adams, she struck a pot-bellied rainbow after the fish first ignored her fly but then turned back to hit it. When the rainbow rewarded us with a shimmering leap, Kelly shouted with delight. "Wow—that was *awesome!*"

Having watched most of the Watts's videos, which they had sent me before my trip, I was familiar with Kelly's unabashed joy in the simple pleasure of hooking and playing a good fish. Connected to a throbbing trout, both she and Jim fairly bubbled with excitement, and their whooping and laughing and general merriment did not always sit well with all viewers. "We've actually had subscribers cancel on us because they complain we laugh too much on the show," said Jim. "But fly-fishing isn't brain surgery and ought to be fun. Anyone who takes the sport so seriously should re-examine his outlook. There's also a great deal of male chauvinism out there, and some men resent Kelly because she's such a competent angler."

He had hit on a point. John Gierach once wrote that every fly fisherman aspires to be an old fart, and it's amazing how many of us succeed. I recalled what the venerable Charley Waterman had said to me in my interview with him a few years before: "Sex is great, but forget it in hunting or fishing." For some male anglers, at least, Kelly Watt's statuesque good looks and manicured nails were at best an annoying distraction.

The spinners kept falling and the trout continued to feed. By noon we'd caught and released ten fish between us, most of them rainbows of three-plus pounds, and the Watts had the footage they'd been hoping for. The next and final day was icing. Although it was just as bright and hot as the others, for reasons we couldn't fathom but blissfully accepted, the fishing busted open and the Bighorn surpassed its reputation as one of the world's premier trout fisheries. The spinners were so thick on the water that they clogged our lines and piled up in thick mats that choked the backwaters. The trout behaved more like bluefish in a feeding orgy, and by the time they finally turned off in midafternoon we'd hooked into more than thirty large fish.

As Kelly might have put it, it was awesome, and I understood why Jim Watt, the gambler, was willing to bet the farm on his problematical venture. The game itself was the reward.

## THIRTEEN

*Bug Man:
Al Caucci of
the Delaware*

Rocking on the porch of his home on the West Branch of the Delaware River, Al Caucci remembered that morning on a Maine pond thirty-five years before as though it were yesterday. It was 1960, and he had come to the little camp in the shadow of Mount Katahdin eager to learn fly-fishing and to catch some trout, but in two days of flailing the water he'd been blanked—a skunking made worse by the sight of brook trout rising all around him, gorging on huge mayflies hatching on the surface.

The camp's owner, a gruff Down-Easter named George, had sold him a few dozen of his standard flies, but the gaudy Parmachenee Belles and other traditional patterns had drawn only the trouts' contempt. At the end of his second day of frustration, Caucci scooped up a handful of mayflies and brought them back to camp.

"OK, where are your *real* flies—the ones that look like these?" he demanded, shoving the bugs under the camp owner's nose.

George apparently thought his guest had yet to pay his dues as a fly fisherman. "I knew you'd be a pain in the neck from the moment I saw you," he said. But under Caucci's prodding, he disappeared into the back room and returned with a cigar box filled with more naturalistic flies—mostly Adamses and Black Gnats—that at least approximated the mayflies on the pond.

"The next morning," Caucci recalled, "I skipped breakfast and went back out there. I swear every cast caught a fish. It convinced me that you've got to find out what the fish are eating and match it."

In the decades since, Al Caucci (pronounced COO-chi) has devoted much of his busy life to learning about the bugs that trout feed on and to passing that knowledge on to other fishermen. He and his longtime partner, Bob Nastasi, are the coauthors of four angling-related books, including *Hatches*, a guide to identifying and imitating mayflies that sold 50,000 copies in twenty years. His fly-fishing school on the West Branch of the Delaware River near Hancock, New York, has introduced thousands to the joy and humiliation of trying to fool a creature with a pea-sized brain into mistaking a wisp of fur and deer hair for food. And he's been a leader in the uphill struggle to protect the upper Delaware, the East's best wild trout fishery.

Caucci also operates a fishing camp on the Delaware, leads guided trips to Montana, and runs a bonefishing school in the Bahamas. For years he managed to do all this on the side, while holding down a full-time position as the chief engineer of a large industrial brush company. Caucci is the sort who thrives on work, but a mild heart attack caused him to rethink his priorities. In February 1995, at age fifty-eight, he quit his daytime job to devote all his time to the business of fishing.

With a persistence and single-mindedness that have often baffled his family, Caucci has been pursuing fish of one type or another since he was a kid growing up in Bristol, Pennsylvania, on the lower Delaware north of Philadelphia. The son of a barber and the oldest of five children, he lived two blocks from the river. The lower Delaware was severely polluted then, but the raw sewage and waste from a local soap factory didn't stop him or his friends from swimming in the river or fishing in it for channel catfish, using chicken guts scrounged from the neighborhood grocer as bait. After high school, Caucci worked as a draftsman while studying mechanical engineering at night. Still he found time for fishing—for bass and pickerel in gravel pits excavated for the building of Levittown, Pennsylvania, and for striped bass and bluefish along the New Jersey shore.

The obsession with fly-fishing came along about the time he got married, at twenty-three. He fished in the nearby Pocono Mountains, where he bought a weekend property on the headwaters of a trout stream. He tied flies and kept an aquarium for observing mayfly nymphs and other aquatic insects, which he identified using the few angling entomology guides then available. In 1969, he met Bob Nastasi through a neighbor and mutual friend. Nastasi worked as an art director for an advertising agency, and like Caucci he was crazy for fly-fishing. The two began fishing together, and before long Nastasi proposed they write a book about fly-fishing for trout. Existing volumes on the subject could have filled a good-sized library, but the would-be coauthors were undaunted: they determined to take a fresh approach by doing their own stream research and creating a new series of fly patterns to imitate mayflies. The book, *Comparahatch,* was published in 1973, and two years later they followed it with *Hatches,* a more ambitious work that built on the first.

Initially marketed by Field & Stream Book Club, *Hatches* offered anglers an easy-to-understand system for identifying mayfly hatches from the Rockies to the Appalachians. To match those hatches, Caucci and Nastasi advocated their Comparadun, a style of dry fly with the virtues of simplicity, ruggedness, and generic bugginess. Adapted from Fran Betters's venerable Haystack, the basic Comparadun is nothing more than a wing of pinched deer hair, a body of dyed rabbit fur, and a pair of widely split tails. Tied in sizes eight to twenty-four with variously colored bodies, it can imitate anything from the biggest Green Drake to the tiniest Blue-Winged Olive. In contrast to traditional dry flies, the Comparadun dispenses with hackle to "cock" the fly on the surface, relying instead on the splayed wing and pontoonlike tails to float it flush in the film. This results, Caucci believes, in a more realistic presentation to feeding fish.

Compiling the data for their two books took three years of intensive research. In a rented motor home converted to a laboratory on wheels—complete with aquarium, seine nets, tape recorders, cameras, maps, notebooks, and scientific references—Caucci and Nastasi assayed streams in the East, Midwest, and West. They collected and photographed the nymphs, duns, and spinners of every mayfly species of importance to trout. By the time they were done, the two amateur bug men may have known more about their subject than any professional entomologist. "We found species that aren't even in the books," said Caucci, when I interviewed him at his fishing camp in 1995 for *Field & Stream.* "Here on the Delaware, for example, we've got six species of Hendrickson, and only two of them have scientific names. They vary in size from twelve to sixteen and in body color from pinkish buff to dark olive and brown. Entomologists look mostly at insects regarded as pests. We've been trying to get them to look at mayflies as indicator species for water quality, but without much success."

Caucci can "talk Latin" when discussing bugs, but he isn't hung up on scientific nomenclature. He tends to call a Hendrickson a Hendrickson, and "Blue-Winged Olive" is good enough for the *Pseudocleon* that comes off the Delaware in summer and fall. Just plain "Sulphurs" suffices for the range of yellowish mayflies that can brighten an angler's afternoon or evening in June or July. "We keep it simple," he says. "I tell our students, You can play this game on the level of chess or checkers, it's up to you. The idea is to have fun. But if you want to be challenged, hatch matching is the way to go."

While doing their field research, Caucci and Nastasi caught, killed, and autopsied the occasional fish to learn what it was feeding on. Otherwise, the pace and pressure left no time for fishing. The work also took a toll on their personal lives. "We were never home," Caucci recalled, "and we never saw our families. We each had a wife and three little kids and were working full-time jobs. Every spare minute of our nights, weekends, and vacations were spent on those books." They dedicated *Hatches* to "our fishing widows . . . and our fishing orphans." Today, Betti Caucci helps Al with his business but leaves the angling to him. Early in their marriage, said Caucci, "I'd take her fishing, and she'd dab her fly for a while. Then I'd noticed she'd be on a rock reading a book, then in the car reading a book. But she's always encouraged me and never complained. When you get as involved as I am with fly-fishing, either your wife goes along with it, you quit, or you wind up in divorce court." The Cauccis had two boys and a girl, all grown and married, and a grandchild. Their older son, Blair, was a partner of Al's and the family's only other fisherman.

Early in my own fly-fishing I spent a year collecting and identifying stream insects, and *Hatches* was my bible. For my profile of Caucci I audited his weekend fly-fishing course at the Delaware River Club, the low-frills fishing camp he operates on the West Branch. This was the last course of the season, and the turnout was light. Of the six students—two father–son pairs and a husband and wife—four were total novices. Assembled at picnic tables next to the casting lawn on a bright Friday morning, they received the gospel from instructor and guide Jim Charron: "We ask that any fish you catch you release unharmed. We get a deep satisfaction out of that, and I'm sure you will too."

Over the next two and a half days, Charron and the two other instructors, Jerry Wolland and Ben Rinker, grounded the students in casting, knot tying, reading the water, and stream entomology, capped by a Sunday morning exercise in identifying bugs using the Caucci-Nastasi *Instant Mayfly Identification Guide*. The charts and photos in this spiral-bound booklet offer the boiled-down essence of *Hatches,* along with a simple key based on characteristics like wing shape and the number of tail fibers.

Charron, Rinker, and I spent a half hour on the river with a seine net and specimen jars, kicking rocks and harvesting an assortment of aquatic bugs for the class. Back at the picnic tables, the students pored over our lilliputian menagerie with magnifying loupes. With tweezers, Wolland singled out a claret-colored critter, which the group quickly identified as some kind of mayfly nymph. Beth Fusco peered at it through her loupe, and with coaching from Wolland began working her way through the identification guide. Keying on clues like color, size, and the placement of gills along the abdomen, within minutes she had the bug identified as an *Isonychia sadleri,* a common summer species often imitated by a Zug Bug. "Notice that its wing case is swollen and dark. That tells us it's ready to hatch and is going to be active," said Wolland. "We group this among the 'swimming' nymphs—to imitate it you've got to fish your fly in short jerks."

Fly fishermen have been debating the relative merits of imitation versus presentation since the days of horsehair lines. Unlike Ed Van Put, Caucci is a firm believer in hatch matching, but he emphasizes that in dry-fly-fishing, how you present your fly to a feeding trout is at least as critical as the fly itself: "If you have the right fly but can't get it to the fish, it's not going to do you much good." Most of the dry-fly-fishing on the upper Delaware is in long riffles, whose broken currents generate drag and make rises hard to see. Caucci's instructors preach the need for a drag-free float and a presentation that doesn't "line" the fish. That means wading into position abreast or slightly upstream of a feeding fish and executing a reach cast: sweep your arm upstream at the same time it is coming down on the forward cast. This throws an upstream mend in the line, absorbing drag, and drops the fly so that it drifts over the trout before the leader. The preferred casting position also puts the sun at the angler's back, making it easier for him to spot the fly while blinding the fish to the angler's presence.

On the surface at least, Al Caucci's hatch matching philosophy couldn't be more different from Van Put's view that presentation is everything. Yet watching Al fish, I was struck by the similarities in his style and Ed's. Like Van Put, when Caucci fishes riffles, he spends more time looking for rises than casting. He keeps on the move, changing the angle of his eyes to the stream's surface to pick up the fleeting rise forms of feeding fish. Once he finds a fish he works it hard, with patience and persistence, changing flies until he hits on the right one. "The best gauge for whether a fly is right is to throw it out on the water," he said. "If it sticks out from the naturals, you're just asking for a refusal. Fish key into the size of the fly, its attitude or silhouette on the water, and the shade of the body, although not necessarily the color, especially at dusk."

The easiest time to catch rising fish, he added, "is at the beginning and end of a hatch. Early in the hatch you'll find a lot of juvenile fish, but as the hatch gets heavier, the bigger fish appear, and a pecking order starts to prevail." Sometimes the best fishing is just after the hatch has ended, when a few large fish may continue to rise sporadically. Usually, said Caucci, they are picking off stragglers and cripples—flies that failed to escape their shucks or whose wings were fatally damaged in the act of hatching.

When he and Nastasi were autopsying fish, recalled Caucci, "we'd pull out the mouth, gullet, and entrails and with a razor slice from one end to the other to see how the fish had been feeding over time." The innards of rainbows typically held a variety of insects, indicating a smorgasbord approach to feeding, while the bugs in brown trout were predominantly the same species. A close look at the contents of a brown trout's intestinal tract revealed a feeding succession as the trout moved from one stage of the hatch to another. "Sometimes you'd notice they had started out taking the duns, then had keyed on the emergers," he said.

The vulnerability of emergers—mayflies struggling in the surface film to escape their nymphal shucks—makes them favorite targets of hungry trout, and one of the more effective Caucci-Nastasi patterns is an emerger with a trailing shuck made of Z-Lon, a translucent synthetic wool. A C-N Emerger held me in good stead on a late afternoon in May 1994, when a Hendrickson hatch was coming off the West Branch and I cast over a pod of feeding fish in water less than a foot deep. In the course of an hour I caught and released three wild brown trout—two of fifteen inches, plus a sixteen-incher. A year later I hit the same pool and stood slack-jawed at the sight of another hatch of Hendricksons, the heaviest I have ever seen. The river was probably fifty yards wide, and every square foot of it appeared covered by duns riding the current like tiny sailboats. Trout were sipping the naturals, but they turned up their noses at everything I offered, including the Comparaduns that had worked the year before.

My skunking was neither the first nor the last I've received on the Delaware, a river whose fecundity has inspired some of its more enthusiastic admirers, including Al Caucci, to hype it as "the Bighorn of the East," as the subtitle of an article in *Fly Fisherman* once described it. It isn't and never will be. The upper Delaware is a good wild-trout fishery that could be better. Like the Bighorn, the Beaverkill, and most of the West's other premier trout rivers, it is a tailwater fishery, nourished by cold water pouring from reservoirs on its West and East Branches. The dams back up reservoirs that supply New York City, 140 miles to the southeast. An agreement between New York state, New Jersey, and Pennsylvania requires the city to maintain some minimum flow in the Delaware, and most of the water it releases comes from the Cannonsville Reservoir on the West Branch; flows are minimal from the East Branch's Pepacton Reservoir, whose purer water, filtered by heavy forest cover, is conserved for drinking. Unfortunately, releases from both reservoirs are controlled by bureaucrats who wouldn't know a trout from a truffle, and the health of the fishery is the last item on their agenda. In severe droughts, as occurred five times between 1984 and 1995, they sometimes shut off the flow to the West Branch entirely, exposing the streambed and decimating aquatic insects and the trout sustained by them. At other times they release too much water, turning the river into a raging sluiceway.

Even if flow regimes were maximized for the benefit of trout, the Delaware would never be a match for the best western tailwaters, which have longer growing seasons (due to more sunlight) and a higher pH. In terms of their temperature and water chemistry, western tailwaters are like giant spring creeks. The tailwater stretches of the Bighorn, the Beaverhead, the Green River, the Frying Pan, and the San Juan all flow over calcium-rich bedrock. This results in a water chemistry that—unlike the Delaware's—is alkaline, supporting a dense growth of weeds, which in turn support a huge biomass of crustacea and aquatic insects for trout to feed on. Statistics compiled by New York state fisheries biologists in the early 1990s suggest that the Delaware's upper main stem may hold 250 trout per mile. Most of these fish concentrate in the riffle sections, whose trout density may be 1,250 per mile—a respectable number, certainly, but a far cry from the 4,000 to 8,000 (or more) trout per mile of the great tailwater fisheries of the Rocky Mountains. The concentration of fish in the West Branch is a good deal higher, especially in the summer, when trout from the main stem and the East Branch are drawn to its cooler waters.

Caucci, who began fishing the upper Delaware in the early 1970s, has worked for years with other anglers and Trout Unlimited to improve its fishery. Their efforts have led to the installation in the Cannonsville Dam of a valve that controls water releases more precisely, and to changes in the formula for flow regimes allowing for the release of more water during droughts. They also convinced officials to stop stocking the West Branch and manage it as a wild fishery, with a portion of it catch-and-release. On the main stem, their lobbying resulted in a lower creel limit and better enforcement of conservation laws (poachers had been known to dynamite pools and poison spawning trout with chlorine bleach).

The upper Delaware is a lovely but fickle lady. I've been fishing it off and on for some twenty-five years and have reluctantly concluded that it's a river on which I'll forever be paying my dues. The point was brought home to me yet again on an outing there with Caucci. I arrived at his place on an August day in 1995 to find the Cannonsville Dam pumping out twice its usual volume for that time of year. The water temperature was in the fifties (ideal for trout), but the weather was hot and sultry, and Al couldn't remember when the fishing had been slower. Blame it on the high water or the unsettled barometer—whatever the reason, the Delaware had gone into a funk, and my own mood followed. In the evening, Caucci took me to a main-stem pool whose sweeping beauty was a compensation of sorts for the utter absence of rising fish. The next morning we scouted for fish dimpling on Tricos, but a heavy fog put off both bugs and trout. Moving up the West Branch, we found cedar waxwings swooping over a heavily fished riffle, taking Sulphurs. A few trout began showing, but my every cast drew a blank.

The hatch ended, and we were wading back upstream when Caucci noticed a couple of sporadic rises. "Sometimes you'll get a little Blue-Winged Olive coming off after the Sulphurs," he said. He gave me a matching Comparadun in size eighteen. My casting put one fish down, but another finally cooperated and took the fly. "He's gonna run on you," said Caucci, and sure enough, the fish took off and slipped the hook.

I got a glimpse of the trout. It wasn't a big one, probably fourteen inches, and barely hinted at the Delaware's potential. In a phone call later, Al told me he had returned to the same riffle the next night and caught two eighteen-inch browns— "big slab-sided fish that took me into backing."

Al Caucci is one of the nicest guys I know, and I begrudged his success for only a moment. Was his river being cruel to me, or merely indifferent?

## FOURTEEN

# Norman Maclean Needn't Have Worried

It was all in a day's work for Craig Sheffer, the young actor who played author Norman Maclean in the film version of *A River Runs through It*, the autobiographical classic about love, death, and fly-fishing. In the climactic scene in both the book and the movie, Norman competes with his brother, Paul, to catch the most fish during a hatch of salmon flies. "Big clumsy flies," Maclean wrote, which "bumped into my face, swarmed on my neck and wiggled in my underwear." During the filming of this sequence, Sheffer stood for two hours surrounded by a camera crew, directors, makeup artists, and the legion of others involved in making a movie, while John Dietch, the coordinator of the film's fly-fishing segments, pelted him with salmon flies—juicy, thumb-sized *Pteronarcys californicas*.

Salmon flies may be beautiful in the eyes of fishermen, Dietch said later, but most of those involved in the film looked on them with an attitude more like revulsion. "Their size shocked people," said Dietch. "When I talked to the screenwriter about this scene, I assumed he knew these bugs were big, but he and a lot of others didn't. They were grossed out."

Dietch, who ordinarily divides his time between guiding near his home in Aspen, Colorado, and making documentary films in Los Angeles, told this story with relish when I spoke to him in late July 1991, in Livingston, Montana. He also recounted how he gave Brad Pitt, the actor who played Paul, his first fly-casting lessons on Malibu Creek, in the heart of Hollywood's beach colony. "Later, we found this dried-up concrete pond in Los Angeles with some children playing around it. To give Brad a sense of playing a fish, we got one of them to pick up his line and run around the pond with it." Later, when Pitt caught his first real trout, on a Montana spring creek, he turned to Dietch with a grin: "Hey, it's just like that little blond kid!"

In the early 1970s, when Norman Maclean began seeking a publisher for his reminiscences about his youth in Montana, one editor returned the manuscript with the observation, "These stories have trees in them." Eventually the manuscript found a home at the University of Chicago Press, which published *A River Runs through It* in 1976. The title story, a novella about a family relationship rooted in a love of fly-fishing, sparkles with a prose as clean as gravel in an alpine stream. In the years between its first printing and the making of the movie version it went through fifteen printings and took on a cultlike following among anglers and other lovers of the outdoors. By then, trees had more friends.

Among the book's enthusiasts was Robert Redford, who in 1980 bought the film rights and then spent the next decade developing the story for the screen. Finally, a year after Maclean's death in 1990, Redford shot the film, which was released in October 1992. During the late phase of the filming, I spent a day and most of one night on location for an article for *Fly Rod & Reel*. I wanted to know how Redford (the director and narrator) and others had resolved two key problems in adapting the story to the screen. One was the unavoidable fact that Maclean's tale has trout in it as well as trees. Trout and fly-fishing are central to the story, but to the average moviegoer, fly-fishing is about as understandable as ikebana, and maybe less interesting. The other problem concerned the story itself: The book is nearly plotless, with none of the dramatic conflict required of a commercial film.

For the three fly fishermen in the world who haven't read or seen *A River Runs through It*, I ought to say a little more about the story and its author, who wrote it in his seventies after retiring as a professor of English at the University of Chicago. Norman Maclean and his younger brother, Paul, grew up in Missoula. They were sons of a Presbyterian minister, a flinty Scot who had come to Montana in the 1890s. The Reverend John Maclean (in the movie played by Tom Skerritt) taught his sons to fly fish, and it was their shared passion for the sport and their home water, the Blackfoot River, that bonded the three of them. "In our family," wrote Maclean in his famous opening sentence, "there was no clear line between religion and fly fishing." The pursuit of trout with a fly became a spiritual quest: in the Reverend's view, "all good things— trout as well as eternal salvation—come by grace and grace comes by art and art does not come easy."

For Paul in particular, the art of fly-fishing became an obsession. So too did cards and booze. Maclean's story is largely about his incandescent brother and the inability of his family to help him. In the end, he is beaten to death in an alley, probably for gambling debts.

Although Paul is a fatally flawed character, his artistry with a fly rod redeems him, and I knew that the movie's credibility would hinge on conveying his mastery of the sport in all its grace and power. To capture the beauty of fly-fishing, Redford hired as his director of photography Philippe Rousselot, whose credits included the outdoor epics *The Bear* and *The Emerald Forest,* as well as *Dangerous Liaisons, Hope and Glory,* and *Henry and June* (his work on the last two had earned him nominations for Academy Awards).

Redford also recruited Dietch, who lined up other angling consultants to teach the rudiments of fly-fishing to the actors (none of whom were fishermen) and to ensure that the period details of tackle and technique were accurate. The American Museum of Fly fishing, the Federation of Fly Fishers, and various commercial vendors supplied vintage rods, reels, and accessories. In the film, each character's equipment reflects his personality and approach to the sport. As the product of a genteel British tradition, for example, the Reverend Maclean goes astream in tweeds, with a Hardy reel and Wheatley fly boxes. Norman's reel is a serviceable Pfleuger, and both he and his father fish with factory-model cane rods by Montague. Paul's outfit is a Hardy and a high-priced Granger rod with a leather case. They fish silk lines—the only kind available before World War II—supplied by Phoenix, a British firm that still makes them. (Silk lines and gut leaders were used in close-ups, but for long shots the actors and doubles relied on modern amber-colored synthetics.) The characters wade wet, in venerable Red Ball wading boots, and they don't wear fishing vests, which didn't come into widespread use until after the war. For the sake of verisimilitude to an era of twenty-fish-per-day limits, they also carry wicker creels that fairly groan under the weight of dead trout. The movie's closing credits include a message promoting catch-and-release.

Jerry Siem, a consultant from the Winston Rod Company, told me that fly fishers accustomed to modern casting technique, with its emphasis on arm work and line speed, would be surprised at the movie's depiction of the more leisurely prewar style of wrist casting, in which the elbow stays locked on the hip. "You won't see people pumping double hauls," he said. "It was a much slower style, with more exacting rod–hand work than today." John Bailey, another consultant and the son of Dan Bailey, noted that Paul had a more aggressive casting style, with more arm casting, than his brother and father. "When I was working with the actors, I told them to think of casting as an extension of their characters. They picked up on that right away."

The ultimate authority on the Macleans as anglers was George Croonenberghs. At the time of the filming Croonenberghs was in his eighties. As a boy he was taught fly tying by the Reverend, and later he fished with the brothers and tied flies for them. A resident of Missoula, he was on hand during the filming of the fishing sequences. In the climactic scene, Paul catches a thirty-inch trout with a Croonenberghs No. 2 Yellow Hackle, fished to imitate a drowned salmon fly. This and most of the other flies used in the film were tied by Croonenberghs.

"George has a great memory, and he's been our best resource for all this," said Dietch. When researching the rods used by the Macleans, Dietch first called Len Codella, a former partner in Thomas and Thomas and an authority on antique tackle. "Len decided their rods were probably Montagues, which were prevalent then and affordable. Later, when I called George to ask if he'd ever heard of MONT-a-guze, he said no. I asked what kind of rods the guys used, and he said 'MONT-ags.'"

The point of the story, Dietch added, is that everyone in Montana probably called them MONT-ags. "Working on this film with George has shown me how localized fly-fishing was, from the kinds of rods and flies people used to the way they threaded their line and connected the line to the leader—basically, it was just with a big old granny knot, which they tied leaving a big tag end. The leader was short, with no butt section. By our standards it was crude fishing." John Bailey agreed. The use of silkworm gut, he said, limited how fine leaders could be. "Gut was very weak. Effectively you couldn't fish much below 3X, which had a breaking strength of about two pounds." By contrast, today's 3X mono breaks at about seven pounds.

Their relatively coarse tackle notwithstanding, the Macleans were innovative fishermen, said Bailey. "Talking with George, it becomes clear that they were very avant-garde for their time. They were using dry flies in Montana in 1936, when nobody out here knew what a dry fly was."

The closest thing to a local dry fly was the Bunyan Bug. Tied by Norman Means, of Missoula, these big, cork-body floaters sport horsehair wings and cast about as easily as bricks. A Bunyan Bug figures prominently in *A River Runs through It* and, working in the back of Bailey's shop, tier Ron Brown created a bunch of them for the movie. Bailey pointed out an anachronism related to the fly's appearance on the screen: Although most of the action in the book takes place in the summer of 1937, the film, for reasons of plot, moves the main part of the story back a decade to 1926—a year before Means tied his first Bunyan Bug.

In other ways as well the filmmakers weren't slavish about sticking to the book's every detail, even while remaining faithful to its spirit and its tackle. The scenes representing downtown Missoula in the 1920s, for example, were actually shot in Livingston, whose East Callender Street was done over for the occasion in period storefronts. In the basement of Livingston's civic center, construction crews built an elaborate set that replicated the interior of the Maclean house in Missoula. And the river sequences that purport to show the Macleans fishing on the Blackfoot were filmed on the Gallatin and Boulder Rivers, which more closely approximate what their home river looked like sixty years before. The Blackfoot watershed, said Dietch, "has terrible clearcuts, with no trees on the upper parts. And the fishery has been severely damaged by siltation."

(Purists concerned about the filmmakers' liberties with Maclean's story should remember that the author, for reasons of narrative, did not always hew to the facts either. For example, Paul died in Chicago, not Helena. And while the novella suggests that he went directly from high school to newspaper work without attending college, he actually enrolled at the University of Montana for two years and then—following his brother, Norman—transferred to Dartmouth College, from which he graduated in 1928.)[1]

When I spoke to Dietch in Livingston, which served as the crew's headquarters, the filming of the climactic fishing scene (shot in Gallatin Canyon, just upstream from Spanish Creek) was still several weeks away. He said that the film's two camera units were scheduled for a total of three to five days of shooting, for what might amount to only three to five minutes on the screen. Patrick Markey, the producer, said the crew would be working with biologists from the Montana fish and game department and from Inter-Fluve, a company that creates and restores trout habitat. "They'll be our trout wranglers, handling the fish for us and doing all our hook-ups and resuscitation, so the fish won't be damaged," he said. The ASPCA would be on hand too, "but more as a collaborator than as a watchdog."

Participants were reluctant to give away too many technical details about how the scene would be shot. "We don't

---

1. For more on the background of the Macleans and Norman's writing techniques, see *Norman Maclean* in the American Authors Series, edited by Ron McFarland and Hugh Nichols (Lewiston, Id.: Confluence Press, 1988).

want to destroy the mystique," said Faith Conroy, a publicist. From one person close to the filming, however, I learned of the mechanical trout that would be used for close-ups of a fish striking a fly.

The effort lavished on the fly-fishing would doubtless have pleased Norman Maclean. His son-in-law, Joel Snyder, who was present on the set, recalled Maclean coming by his house after publication of *A River Runs through It*. "He had a big grin on his face and quoted from a review in a fishing magazine he had with him: 'Maclean doesn't make *one error* of fact about fly-fishing.' Then he threw the magazine down on the table and said, 'Now that's what I call an A-plus review!'"

"So, yeah," Snyder added, "he'd have been very concerned about authenticity, and what Redford has done with the fly-fishing has been wonderful to see. But he promised Norman it would be this way, and he's kept his promise."

A professor of literary and visual studies at the University of Chicago as well as a professional photographer, Snyder shot the "period" family photographs used as props at the beginning of the film. Jean Snyder, Joel's wife and Maclean's daughter, was also on hand as a consultant for much of the shooting. And their son, Jake, who had just completed his freshman year of college, worked on the catering crew and wangled a bit role as a piano player in a speakeasy. (His one line: "And now, the muskrat ramble. . . .") Jake boasts the distinction of having learned fly-fishing from his grandfather. "He taught me just the way his father taught him," he said, "and on the Blackfoot."

Joel Snyder also fly fishes but admitted to slinging hardware too. "I'm rather eclectic," he said, and the same was true of his father-in-law: "Norman told me he fished with Dardevles in the thirties, and as a kid fishing with bait he had real killer instincts. He'd take a live frog, hook it under the throat, float it out into the river on a shingle, then yank it off the shingle and watch it disappear into the maws of a big trout. There was no art in that."

Snyder told me this while the two of us watched the crew preparing for filming. We were in the hills north of Bozeman, where an old ranch building had been gussied up to look like the seedy hot springs resort where Paul goes to gamble. It was night, and big reflector screens had been set up on the hill to throw indirect light on the set. A Model T Ford was parked in front of the building, and the crew was laying track for the camera dolly. Pitt and Sheffer were in costume, glaring intently from beneath fedoras as they readied for one of the film's crucial scenes, in which Paul introduces Norman to his underworld. Redford, in blue jeans, an old high school letter jacket, and a rakish silk scarf, with a tweed cap like the one he wore in *The Sting* tilted jauntily on his golden head, conferred with the actors and checked camera angles.

He had waited eleven years to make this film. Convincing Maclean that he could successfully adapt his story to the screen had been a hard sell, but over time Redford had won the old man's trust and, shortly before his death, Maclean approved an early draft of the script. In a brief conversation I had with Redford—in honesty I can't call it an interview—he referred to Maclean as "monomaniacal." He said it with a smile, and it was obvious that he'd developed an affection for the crusty author during their long negotiation. Yet I couldn't help wondering if he would be filming now if Maclean still lived. In an earlier telephone conversation I had with the author's son, John, he had spoken of the "polka dance" between Redford and his father over artistic control. And John Bailey, who knew Maclean in the last years of his life—he was the second recipient of the Dan and Helen Bailey Memorial Award, which honors contributors to fly-fishing—recalled his grousing, "They're trying to make this movie, but I don't think they'll get it right."

A key person charged with "getting it right" was the screenwriter Richard Friedenberg, whom Redford hired in 1988 on the basis of his Emmy-winning TV script for *Promise,* another story of brotherly love. Friedenberg was present throughout the filming, revising the script as needed, and I had a chance to talk with him about the difficulty of adapting the book. "Norman didn't tell a full story, and as a novelist—unlike a screenwriter—he didn't have to," he said. "His novella is 104 pages, 52 of which are about fly-fishing, so there's very little story there. I had to find a way to tell a full story that didn't violate Norman's intentions."

In the book, Friedenberg noted, Norman is in his thirties, married, and launched on an academic career. He's an observer more than a participant in the story, "and I had to find a period when his life had drama." After talking to Maclean himself and to members of his family, Friedenberg decided to move the story back a decade, to the 1920s, when the future author was still at loose ends about his future. He had graduated from Dartmouth College and had stayed there to teach and write for a couple of years. Then he returned to Montana, undecided whether to pursue a Ph.D. in literature or a career in the U.S. Forest Service. "He just sort of hung out, not doing much—it was very modern," said Friedenberg.

This was also when Maclean began courting Jessie, his future wife, and Friedenberg used their relationship to introduce a romantic element into the story. A minor and rather featureless character in the book, she is fleshed out considerably in the movie. Her part is played by Emily Lloyd, a British actress who specializes in American roles.

The real Jessie, said Friedenberg, had a wild streak and in temperament resembled Paul more than his sober-sided brother. Friedenberg read letters that Paul had written to

Jessie prior to her marriage, letters that were "much more poetic and beautiful than Norman's. He called them a threesome—'Three against the world.' I think he loved her very, very much, as his brother's intended, and he also recognized that Jessie was very much more like himself than like Norman."

Like everyone who's read *A River Runs through It*, Friedenberg and others involved in the film were captivated by the central character. "I *love* Paul," said Brad Pitt, who played him. "Paul jumps—he challenges everything." Said Friedenberg, "Paul had a real darkness. This story is about a lot of things but ultimately it's about his strange, inexplicable darkness and his inability to stop himself in his slide toward death. His character remains inexplicable, although it's clear he was an addictive guy."

Fly-fishing, of course, was Paul's "good" addiction. As for its role in the film, said Friedenberg, "my take on it right away was that less is more. I wanted the fly-fishing sequences to be honest and beautiful, but they have to advance the story and reveal as much as any other scenes about the characters."

He added that the film's editors would ultimately decide how much fly-fishing appeared on the screen. Whether it was less or more didn't seem important to me. What mattered was the integrity that Redford and company were investing in the film as a piece of art in which every part is integral to the whole. Norman Maclean needn't have worried.

# *Postscript*

Dan Bailey died in 1982, but his fly shop (www.dan-bailey.com) has expanded under the management of his son, John.

Fran Betters still operates the Adirondack Sport Shop (518-946-2605), and through its Web site (www.aus-ablewulff.com) he makes available the books he's written over the years on the Adirondacks and fishing. They include *Fran Betters' Ausable River Guide, Fishing the Adirondacks, Fran Betters' Fly Tying and Pattern Guide, Fish Are Smarter in the Adirondacks,* and *Something's Fishy in the Adirondacks* (poems and fish stories).

Dennis Black in 1998 sold his controlling interest in Umpqua Feather Merchants to his son Jim, insider Nick Murphy, and a group of outside investors. He remains active in the business, overseeing Umpqua's Asian factories, and he owns

Feather Merchants International, a firm that wholesales flies to countries other than the United States. Black divides his time between homes on the North Umpqua—where he spends summer and fall, fishing the steelhead run—and in New Zealand, where he spends our winter and spring fishing for trout.

Al Caucci continues to expand his Delaware River Club. Its Web site (www.mayfly.com) offers an on-line catalog and reports on fishing conditions.

Chuck Fothergill died of prostate cancer on May 13, 1995, at age sixty-three.

Joe Humphreys, now seventy-one, took early retirement from Penn State in 1989, a year after I interviewed him. The course taught by Joe and founded by George Harvey continues to be taught. Since Joe left teaching, he's completed *On the Trout Stream with Joe Humphreys* (Stackpole, 1989; photos by Boyd Pfeiffer) and an updated version of *Joe Humpreys's Trout Tactics* (Stackpole, 1993). He has also produced two videos available through Orvis—*A Casting Approach to Nymph Tactics* and *A Casting Approach to Dry-Fly Tactics in Tight Brush*—and has consulted for Cortland in the development of fly lines. In September 1999 he was a member of the U.S. team in the Worldwide Trout Open, a tournament held in Ireland. The Americans finished eighth out of sixteen countries represented—entirely respectable, given the quality of professional match fishermen in Europe.

Ken Reinard is still doing his shtick as the Colonial Angler, making presentations to fishing clubs and at the annual fly-fishing show in Somerset, New Jersey, where I first met him. His book, *The Colonial Angler's Manual of Flyfishing and Flytying,* was published in 1995 by Fox Chapel (1-800-457-9112).

Al Troth now leaves the rigors of guiding to his son, Eric, but continues to tie flies commercially for his old clients. In November 1991, thirteen months after our float and a few months before my article on him appeared in *Fly Rod & Reel,* Al felt a tightness in his chest and checked himself into a hospital, where the doctors caught a heart attack just in time. He had triple-bypass surgery, lost some forty pounds (while eating an astonishing number of bran muffins), and decided it was time at last to slow down. "They used to say I was a mix of Mr. Rogers and Attila the Hun," he told *FR&R* editor Silvio Calabi. "Now I'm more Mr. Rogers." When I talked with him on the phone recently, he was listening to a jazz tape and making a shadow box of his flies; with typical precision he told me he'd done 380 shadow boxes since his first one in 1981. "They sell without any advertising." He's still proud of his claim of originating the Elkhair Caddis and chuckled to read in a recent book that it had been originated "by the late Al Troth": "It makes you think what Mark Twain said about rumors of his demise being greatly exaggerated."

Ed Van Put still fishes the upper Delaware, but increasingly the river's trout compete for his interest with the wild turkeys on the ridge behind his house.

Charley Waterman, now in his mid-eighties, continues to write for various outdoor magazines, including *Gray's Sporting Journal* and *Fly Fishing in Salt Waters*. A few years ago he and Debie gave up their annual round-trip to Livingston, Montana, and are now based year-round in De Land, Florida.

Jim and Kelly Watt are still traveling around the world making fly-fishing videos. Their work appears regularly on *ESPN Outdoors*. *Fly Fishing Video Magazine* and its parent company, Bennett/Watt Entertainment, based in Issaquah, Washington, can be accessed via the magazine's Web site (www.ffvm.com).

Bill Yellowtail left the Montana senate in 1993 to work for the Clinton administration as a Denver-based regional director in the Environmental Protection Agency. He took a leave in the spring of 1996 to run for Montana's single congressional seat. Following his defeat, he returned to the same position with the EPA. He can now be reached by phone.

# About the Author

J. I. (Jim) Merritt is the author of two books—*Baronets and Buffalo: The British Sportsman in the American West* (Mountain Press, 1985) and *Goodbye, Liberty Belle: A Son's Search for His Father's War* (Wright State University Press, 1993)—and editor of *The Best of Field & Stream* (Lyons & Burford, 1995). He is the editor of *We Proceeded On,* the quarterly journal of the Lewis and Clark Trail Heritage Foundation. He has written more than 160 magazine articles on fishing and the outdoors, natural history, the American West, and other subjects for publications such as *Fly Rod & Reel, Fly Fisherman, Saltwater Fly Fishing, American Angler, American Fly Fisher, Flyfisher, Modern Maturity, People, Bird Watcher's Digest, Sierra, Underwater Naturalist, Archaeology, Americana,* and the *Princeton Alumni Weekly.* He is a contributing editor for *Field & Stream.*

Merritt served in the navy during the Vietnam era, worked five years as a reporter and an editor at *The Press* of Atlantic City, New Jersey, and twenty-four years in various jobs at Princeton University (from which he graduated in 1966), including the editorship of its alumni magazine. He lives in Pennington, New Jersey.